# So, Why Gin?

*One Man's Journey Into the Spirits Business*

by
AJ Temple

So, Why Gin?

White Mule Press a division of the
American Distilling Institute
PO Box 577
Hayward, CA 94541
distilling.com/books

Copyright 2019 © A.J. Temple

All rights reserved.

ISBN 978-1-7322354-2-7

# Contents

| | |
|---|---|
| vii | Preface |
| 3 | Dry Gin |
| 13 | DSP or DNF? |
| 19 | You're Running a Plant |
| 27 | Nuts & Bolts |
| 43 | Some Folks You'll Want to Be Friendly With |
| 51 | Think Forward, Work Backwards |
| 55 | Production Day |
| 69 | A Day of Many Hats |
| 77 | Bitter Aftertaste? |

So, Why Gin?

*We don't kid around about this being a family business, even at two years old Thomas is already eager to help AJ bottle gin, making sure he picks the best corks.*

# Preface

It was love at first sight. And smell. A wide cellar-like room enveloped me, the low ceilings accentuated by large wood beams the color of oak trees in a dark, dense forest. Those beams commanded you to crouch, the room appearing smaller than it was due to their disproportionate size and presence just above your line of sight. My eyes fell on a multitude of heavy burlap sacks that looked like they should be holding soil or grain but the smells around me, permeating my nostrils, said otherwise. It was a sweet, slightly pungent smell that reminded me of the dry, aromatic soil of the Pacific Northwest. When it's dry—a rare occurrence in our neck of the woods—the perfume from the ground as it is kicked up is dominated by evergreen and pine needles.

It was hot in that room and strangely humid for a climate known for being dry. Dry, too, was the product being distilled just above us. Gin. I fell in love with you before I even knew you. Those sacks were filled with juniper berries, kept in storage until the master distiller was ready for another run and would begin shoveling—yes, shoveling—the juniper into the ancient copper pot still.

The still itself was not a gleaming piece of art. I've seen many different stills over the years, some I believe belong in galleries next to works by Chihuly where others … let's just say I wouldn't be too comfortable running them over an open flame. The beauty in this particular still came from history and function. Not just because it had been around for centuries, but it was clearly well used and well loved. We can all browse the web and find and buy new cookware for less than it would cost to pay someone to mow your lawn. Those pots and pans will undoubtedly function as they should—performing their duties of boiling and searing in an efficient, clinical manner. Unlike a stainless fry pan, this copper still has more in common with that ancient cast-iron Dutch oven—one that's seen its share of risotto and Osso Buco over the years. The copper is slightly dull, the shape of it like a bitter onion precariously leaning against your windowsill. The bulbous bottom gives way to the column that is beautifully curved and runs up and across, disappearing into the rear wall of the distillery.

After touring the storage room and production floor—feeling the heat of the still in the air and the smell of juniper and citrus lingering in my nostrils—I believe we ended with a drink. For me it would be a Schweppes Bitter Lemon on ice, unfortunately sans gin (although this is a wonderful combination if you haven't tried it). Here I found myself at the Plymouth Gin distillery, only twelve years old and thousands of miles away from home. Little did I know a seed had been planted. The image of the cellar and subsequent glimpse of the still were the two things that lingered the longest in my mind—the two that have survived the passing of time and rearranging of hazy memories over the years. And Schweppes Bitter Lemon—God, that stuff is amazing even after all these years. Possibly it's because we can't easily find it on this side of the pond, or maybe that's just part of the magic. Travel brings you new flavors, always; it's like seasoning for the soul. That might be why I love gin so much. It's made in almost every corner of the world now, yet you could spend your life traveling and tasting and never find two exactly alike.

I would grow up and go to college. I started out in engineering because of my mechanical background working with cars and just about anything that could be taken apart and put back together. I thought this was the career path I wanted to take. That was until we had a guest speaker from Boeing that proudly talked about the last thirty years of his career designing the left opening flap for the front landing gear on a 737. Kill me now! I'd rather rake leaves for the rest of my life. I'm the kind that doesn't measure seasonings as I cook; it's all based on taste and intuition. If you told your supervisor that the number and placement of rivets on a commercial airplane was determined because it just 'looked right', you'd likely be out of work before the sun went down. Not to say I don't practice the art of precision—that comes with skills only developed over time—but there is a line between precision and art and it's one I try to muddy as often as possible, a practice that just doesn't fit into a mechanical career path like that.

Business administration and marketing it was then, I'll leave engineering to the engineers. I spend far too much time during commercial breaks criticizing television ads for their stark lack of coherent thought—and sometimes the annoyance is the point—so I knew my brain was wired for marketing. My future wife happened to be taking the same courses as well (which I'm sure had nothing to do with the about-face change of major halfway through my sophomore year). We were high-school sweethearts and fairly inseparable, showing up to classes on my rebuilt '91 Honda CBR motorcycle thinking we were the coolest kids on campus. Given the bike was rattle-canned black and some fairings were held together by zip ties—the result of a facelift after I crashed it learning how to ride in the parking lot of our dormitory—it's safe to assume we were somewhat less cool than we thought. When you really want to achieve something, you dust yourself off and get back on the saddle. I believe there's a business lesson in there somewhere—whether it's intelligence or stupidity will only be determined over the course of time. Jamie (my soon-to-be wife) and I dreamed, as starry-eyed youths do, of opening our own business. Of what kind we had no idea.

Ever the gearhead, during and after college I would spend a decade in the automotive industry, managing all aspects of customer service, sales, and work-flow management in a small but very busy independent shop. I loved the business and the people I worked with but knew I couldn't last doing this the rest of my life. The industry is tough. No one wants their cars to have problems, the hours were long *(or so I thought)*, and I knew that if I wanted to make a change it needed to be soon. An old service advisor I worked with passed along a saying about the industry that I found humorous yet haunting at the same time. When asked "How far away do you live from your job?" he would pause—considering the question—then respond with "about four beers." The average career span was roughly four years at a single location before an advisor would either get burnt out and switch paths or move to a different spot, foolishly thinking the next time would be different. I was more the former—a level of burnout present and an internal clock ticking away on the time I had to make a risky move. A move such as opening a gin distillery.

That seed was still in the soil of my brain, just waiting for some water and sunlight to grow. I've been destroying the kitchen since I got my first cookbook around the age of five. No, I wasn't a child prodigy. In fact, my fourth-grade cooking presentation resulted in pieces of the plastic bag from a box of brownie mix being baked into the final product. Not my idea of added flare, nor did it bode well for our final grade. My mother still brings it up from time to time—usually when brownies are being cooked, because we still can't find a recipe better than the one on the back of the Ghirardelli Double Chocolate Brownie box. That aside, I spent a lot of my youth perfecting my palate, watching and observing my parents and their good friends prepare all sorts of different, delicious cuisines. We'd spend one evening

# Preface

gathering clams and oysters from the beach at our cabin, steaming the clams and baking the oysters with a mixture of bread crumbs, Parmesan, and seasonings including pepper mash from the Tabasco factory on Avery Island. The next evening was an adventure in Jambalaya and maybe something with a Japanese influence the following day. Food, like gin, can take on many forms.

I was also lucky enough to travel quite a bit, which meant I was exposed to a melting pot of food and culture. The result was an obsession with layering flavors, sourcing the best ingredients, and mastering different kitchen tools. This focus was only amplified when I dove into the cocktail scene in my twenties. The cocktail is another medium in which flavors can be manipulated and ingredients and tools matter greatly. It was "quick gourmet cooking" as far as I was concerned—a way to integrate all different levels of umami into one glass and cater that to whomever I was serving. One thing I learned over time in the kitchen is that you have to know when to be **bold**, and when to be *subtle*. My early years consisted of intense levels of seasoning—too many habaneros in the risotto, and smoked ribs with far too much sauce and salt. I was the guy asking the vendor at the spice shop in Pike Place Market if he had any more of that hot sauce he kept underneath his front counter. He did, I loved it, and I think it resulted in a few of my friends taking a break from spicy food for an extended period of time. There's just something magical about hitching a ride to the city and "scoring" a bag of pepper sauce that was too strong for the regular customer! I guess I was a special brand of teenager and cooking with family kept me (moderately) out of trouble.

I am a proud first generation distiller. Chapter One—our brand name—has a lot of different meanings for us but the simplest is just that: this is the first chapter of our story. Over time I developed an intense appreciation for the raw ingredients, the "base" if you will, and the importance of showing respect to that base. For a steak it's the marbling of the tenderloin, for fish it's to use its beautiful skin to pan sear and impart a dense, uninhibited flavor into the meat, and for cocktails it's the gin. It's always been the gin. So, when I was in the midst of a quarter-life crisis with no idea what I was going to do and my wife asks, "If you could do anything, what would it be?" I didn't hesitate.

"Open a gin distillery." The words just fell out of my mouth. I think they surprised me more than they did her, as did her response. I remember almost no hesitation. She looked at me and said, "That's a great idea. Can we do it?" The rest is history.

I love my wife. We are that lucky breed that actually work well together and realize each other's own strengths and weaknesses. She had a background helping run several family businesses, I had the passion and palate to make what's in the bottle. I hadn't thought much, at least to my knowledge, about our family visit to Plymouth all those years back, but I always had that answer keyed up to the question of what I'd do if I won the lottery. We were young, the barriers to entry into the distilling industry were all lessening across the country, and we decided to write a business plan. I knew we wanted to do dry gin—I mean *properly* dry—using a neutral spirit base like many gin distilleries in Europe and the UK. It's not as common a practice in the U.S., especially by smaller distilleries, and I'll explain the differences in greater detail in the first chapter. Through tasting every new gin that was coming to market my palate was getting a bit burnt out on the contemporary, Western gins with lots of grain character and odd, sometimes far too overbearing botanical bills. I wanted to make a classic gin where the botanicals were treated right—not going overboard—starting at "chapter one" of the gin playbook: juniper, citrus, earth, and spice.

# Preface

I wrote this book to help others who find themselves contemplating getting into this wonderful and stressful business. I put those adjectives in that order for a reason. It really is a wonderful industry to be a part of, but it doesn't come without stress. I hope that some of the information I'm providing will help put you at ease, provide direction, sprout new questions otherwise not thought of, and help you avoid any pitfalls that may come your way. Bill Owens, president of the American Distilling Institute, asked me to write this book when he paid me a visit in 2018. He was impressed with our setup—making a small warehouse work in an efficient manner—and wanted a snapshot of "a day in the life" of a distiller like myself with two little kids at home and the ambition to make this work. It's easy to write about one specific day, but I constantly find that not one day is the same as the next. I'll call this more of a handbook in dry gin distillation, with our personal experiences interwoven throughout.

The short version? It can be done. In three and a half years of being open we've received 22 awards for our four gins and our gin-based limoncello, we're distributed in four states (and Belgium, but that's a story for another day) and are currently working on several more. I've met a lot of industry friends along the way, we're paying rent and are close to those first official paychecks, and I have zero regrets.

Again, it can be done. And if it turns out not to be? We'll just add a "1" and sell all of our remaining bottles of gin as Chapter 11 at a greatly discounted rate. It's always good to have a backup plan, right? Cheers!

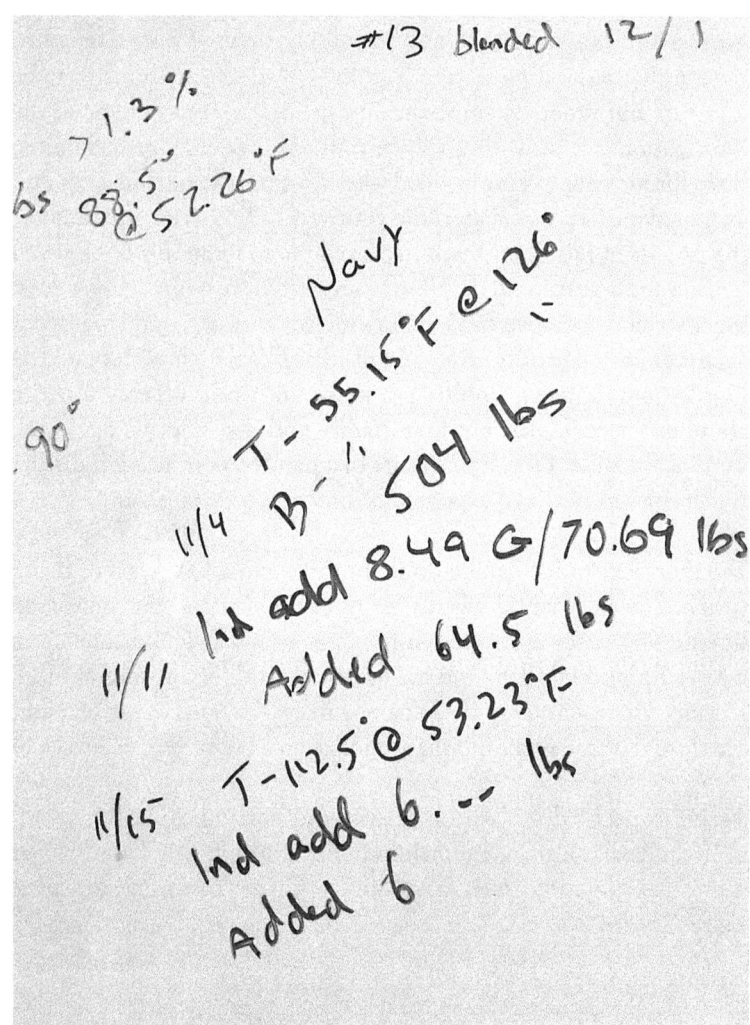

*Getting still-strength gin to final proof is a chore, steps must be taken as water is added to make sure the final measurements are perfect. Our whiteboard sees a lot of ink, this particular day we are proofing some navy strength gin.*

# Dry Gin

How can a liquid be dry? How many Negronis have you had already this morning?

If you haven't heard of a Negroni, please drop everything and go to any bar nearby and ask for one; the book will be here when you get back. Trust me on this one. Secondly, liquid—our gin, for example—can be classified as dry, even if you get a little carried away and spill half your drink down the front of your shirt. While you may not *feel* dry, the term I'm referring to is a character and flavor designation, one that is usually achieved by distilling with a 190-proof neutral spirit as the base.

Our choice to use a grain neutral spirit is one that I'm not ashamed to advertise or talk about. Many distillers in the U.S. do everything in-house from mashing and fermenting to distilling and aging. For small distilleries running equally small stills, this typically means their vodka isn't refined to a "true" neutral, meaning it has residual flavor and character. Vodka is where all gin gets its start; it's the (supposedly) blank canvas used to create your favorite juniper-laced spirit. By using a lesser-refined vodka to re-distill into gin, the gin carries the flavor and mouthfeel from the vodka in addition to whatever botanicals the distiller chooses to add during distillation. This can be due to still size, the fermentation method, and personal preference among other factors. The base spirit flavor may also carry through more heavily by the use of a gin basket, which hangs the botanicals in the path of the vapor in the still—a practice commonly used by craft distilleries who are making vodka and whiskey in the same still and don't want residual botanical oils to cross over into other products. I'm not a vodka guy, but when I do drink it, I actually prefer the ones with some residual flavor, even though that technically isn't the point—and, really, violates the definition—of vodka.

If you aren't familiar with distillation and how spirits are made, let me give you a quick breakdown as it's not as daunting as one would think. In order to create alcohol, you have to feed yeast. Yeast feed on sugars—generally sugars from fruit or sugars that have been converted from starches such as corn or wheat—and the byproduct of that feeding cycle is alcohol. Fermentation will yield an alcohol content anywhere between 5% and 15% (roughly) alcohol by volume. This is where beer and wine end their journey before being bottled or put into barrels. In order to get percentages higher than that such as in distilled spirits, the alcohol needs to be concentrated. Alcohol boils at a lower temperature than water, so by heating it up, the alcohol will boil and turn into a vapor before the water does. A still is essentially a big heater, boiling the alcohol and then cooling that vapor back down at the other end to capture the concentrated boozy molecules. There is a lot more to it when you factor in the different types of alcohol that are produced by fermentation and then the application of things like reflux in a column still, but this is the very crude and basic process of distillation. Vodka is the most refined spirit that a still will produce, the goal being to collect only the pure ethanol molecules to then add water to, creating an odorless and tasteless spirit.

I recently sat on a tasting panel for a regional spirits competition—the first time I had been invited—and I was glad to see several other local distillers there as well. We're in the industry and arguably more involved in tasting straight spirits on a day-to-day basis, so it made sense to have a wide field of judges to lend balance. Our particular table was comprised of four people: myself and a whiskey barrel blender, along with two local bar program managers. Our first flight was vodka. Wonderful.

We silently smelled, tasted, spit, repeated. Our scores and notes made, the discussion opened to ensure we were all on the same page and no review was needed on any of the samples. This is common practice as sometimes palate fatigue or sample size can briefly affect someone's tasting impression. If the majority of the other judges rated differently, it may prompt a re-tasting. You don't have to change your score if you still believe it's great (or crap), but sometimes you can get caught off guard with an initial taste. What proceeded was quite interesting. Our table lead—a local bar manager—started by naming her two best candidates among the six or seven samples and listing off her ratings of each one. The other bar manager was murmuring his agreement. Meanwhile my eyes scanned the table and found those of our whiskey specialist. He and I shared a glance that could only be described as surprised but *not*, bewildered that we could both be so off the mark.

Our answers were nearly opposite from the other half of our team. Not just by a small margin. A lot. To us, the vodka that just tasted like watered-down ethanol was terrible. Likely because that's truly what it was—and, frankly, what most commercial vodka is around the globe. I know the term "ethanol" really takes the romantic wind out of the sails of a product that relies so heavily on marketing, but there it is for you. The whiskey specialist and I preferred the vodkas that had a little bit of character—the ones that tasted like a spirit with more than one dimension. If the vodka was wheat based, I found the soft, hay-like flavor note on the finish playful—my mind going to the kinds of cocktails it could actually lend something to besides just boosting alcohol content. I mean, how on earth can you rate the nose of an ethanol-derived vodka? Is "nothing" worth five points or one? This spurred an interesting discussion, as we all agreed on the taste profiles of every sample, we just couldn't figure out what our judging criteria was supposed to be. If I wanted a vodka to make a vodka tonic that would taste only like tonic, then yes, I'd pick one of the boring ones. If I wanted a vodka with a little character to pair in an espresso martini (I highly recommend one with a grape spirit base), I'd pick one of the others. Banished to a desert island, I'd take the wheat vodka. (Actually, scratch that, I'd take the neutral stuff and try to make a still with coconuts or something. Then I could make a gin with a tropical terroir and market it to passing cruise-line passengers.)

Contrary to some of my previous sentiments, I do believe vodka is very important. Well, to gin that is. Ironically, the vodka I see as pointless on its own is the one I choose to make gin with every day because the result post-distillation is a truly dry gin. We love dry gin. Dry. This term refers to the mouthfeel and body of the spirit more than the actual flavor profile, and to achieve this the base spirit needs to be as pure as possible. To achieve a neutral base spirit—whether distilled from corn, wheat, grapes, etc.—you need a very large and efficient rectification column. This can be achieved on a smaller still, but the yield and time investment required is far from ideal. The added equipment expense, warehouse space, and overall cost would be much more as well.

The reality is that if I were to distill my own vodka, I'd spend three-quarters of my time—thousands of hours each year—breaking my back to make a spirit that is odorless, tasteless, and flavorless, only to put it back in the still and make the gin I set out to make in the first place. Now, I'm not saying sourcing neutral spirit is the only way to go. Every operation and vision of a perfect gin is different. There are countless gins and distilleries I adore that use different base spirits and sometimes funky methods of gin production. They balance those flavors with their botanical selections and do a fantastic job of supporting local grain growers by purchasing all the raw ingredients for fermentation. For us our influence was from across the pond, and unlike the U.S., the European Union actually requires that "distilled gin" be made from a completely neutral spirit base of at least 96% ABV (alcohol by volume). This can certainly be achieved starting at fermentation with a number of different kinds of stills, but unless you are starting with a massive budget, it is hard to do on a consistent basis without that large initial investment of both capital and time. Purchasing a base neutral spirit from a supplier who specializes in making grain neutral spirits ensures consistency and quality.

Some may argue that not starting from a raw grain is not "craft," that it's cheating somehow, and there are endless arguments about how to define craft in a world of growing distilleries and a flood of marketing efforts as a result. Words like *artisan, hand-crafted,* and *small batch* are being used in every corner of the proverbial marketplace. Large companies have paid to run marketing studies, the results showing that consumers place additional value onto products that use those terms. So, where does that leave you as a consumer, when you see the word *artisan* stamped on your bottle of gin but also on that off-colored pack of lunch meat in the "managers special" discount bin at your local grocery store?

As I write this, I have a bottle of gin on my counter—a popular West Coast botanical gin that I won't name—that markets itself as "handcrafted" and presumably small batch due to the handwritten batch and bottle numbers on the front label. The problem? It's batch number 44, but the bottle number is 26,947. *Small* batch? Kudos to whoever the poor bastard was that had to hand write those labels!

## So, Why Gin?

At the end of the day, I'm proud of our product, and as long as it doesn't taste like vodka (which trust me, it certainly does not), it means we drastically changed it from where it began—taking a tasteless blank canvas and painting our flavors onto it, creating our gin. To me that can mean craft or whatever term you prefer, but I believe it's important to be transparent and open about it, even if we're just discussing the part of our gin that shouldn't have an impact on what you're tasting in the first place.

Dry gin is all about the botanicals; they make up the majority of the taste you experience since their oils are the only thing being infused into that base spirit. Most would argue that gin should have lots of juniper, and U.S. law requires it to be the "main characteristic flavor." Juniper, however, is not a very strong ingredient compared to others like citrus peel and cardamom. You're going to be using ten or a hundred times the juniper by weight than some other ingredients, and that leaves a lot open in terms of flavor development. You could cut back your juniper by 90%—staying within the legal range as it will still be the primary ingredient by weight—and end up with a gin that has relatively no juniper flavor. At the time of my writing there is a large overseas gin maker who started a campaign against "fake gin"—partly a dig at our current political and perceived media issues here at home but mostly against the distilleries who are supposedly muddying the proverbial gin waters by releasing gins that taste nothing like the juniper that's used to define them. Gin's origins stretch back centuries, with recording of juniper being infused into alcohol from as far back as A.D. 70 for medicinal purposes. The Dutch have been making jenever—a malt wine spirit flavored with juniper berries—for centuries, the name derived from the Latin *juniperus*. From those and the French word *genièvre* came the modern shorthand term *gin*, underlining the fact that gin's main ingredient is part of its history and identity in a huge way.

# Dry Gin

There have been so many unique gins coming out as of late that another large vodka manufacturer (notice my use of that word versus *distiller*) recently launched a series of "botanical" vodkas aimed at consumers who are jumping ship from their vodka and going over to these new styles of gin, previously deterred due to the juniper aspect that is now almost non-existent in some offerings. I've only ever met people who have told me they "used to be vodka drinkers" and have since seen the light and switched to gin. Never once have I heard someone going the other way and leaving gin for vodka, so I found this new product line quite interesting from a marketing perspective. It's a crude term to some, but technically gin is simply a flavored vodka, the flavor being derived through distillation rather than through an additive put in after the fact—and through, of course, juniper, always the main character, at least in our story.

I could ramble on for pages about my opinions on gin flavor balance, the use of certain botanicals, distillation techniques, cocktail applications, etc. It's what I absolutely love about gin: There are no two that taste the same, and the sky's the limit for what you want your gin to be. One piece of advice that I'll give is to use more than two botanicals, but for the love of God please use fewer than twenty. Maybe twenty-five. My palate is quite good—I've picked eighteen out of twenty gins in a blind tasting (essentially only missing the mark on one, and I'll go ahead and blame that on palate fatigue)—but many average consumers aren't as dialed in to nuanced flavors. Or they just don't care as much, grabbing gin to immediately toss into a cocktail with five other overpowering ingredients. I recently held a botanical tasting class at the distillery and gave folks five botanicals and five numbered distillates—all pure extractions of their respective ingredients. I thought I may have made it too easy using just juniper, lemon peel, cardamom, coriander, and angelica. All have good naked fragrance, all are common in many London Dry gins, and none are too close in flavor to one another. Out of my entire class, no one got all of them correct. That was five, imagine what many consumers would experience with twenty-five.

Another word of advice: Start by making distillates. Plural. Select botanicals you know and ones you don't, distill them on a tabletop still—many can be had for less than $300—and taste them often. Blend them, learn how they interact with each other and how each fits your vision of a gin. Don't even think about making compound batches (a blend of all your botanicals) until you've become familiar with your ingredients and understand how each one reacts during distillation. Treat them like spices in your kitchen, learning which ones play well together and which ones don't. Research other gins and find their botanical bills (when possible), and treat those like a store-bought spice mix, seeing how each element complements one another. Does that orange peel taste better added right before turning on the still or with an overnight maceration to extract its lighter oils when cold? Is lemon verbena good when distilled over high heat? (Hint: the answer is no. Seriously, I'll just save you the trouble on that one.) Did you know that grains of paradise have an almost lavender-like nose after distillation yet very little smell or flavor when raw? Play around with starting ABV and then start adjusting your final ABV to see how you like the oil suspension in each one.

This part took up months of our lives (very busy but enjoyable months) and the result was that we created a gin we love. We learned so much about botanicals and their flavors at different alcohol levels that while the London Dry gin took six months to perfect, our Navy Strength variation only took one try. We knew what we wanted it to be—a citrus forward and punchy big brother to our flagship gin—and our experience with our botanicals and equipment, plus perhaps some blind luck, resulted in a gin we love just as much as the flagship

London Dry. We've been using the same recipe ever since and incidentally we sell just as much of the latter gin as the former, despite thinking the Navy gin was going to be more of a one-off spirit for us.

Work hard, love your products and what you do, and it will rub off on others. This is simply a summation of what we believe and have learned about dry gin, and a call to go make your own, dry or not.

So, Why Gin?

*Ingredients matter, and with gin the juniper is king. These are whole juniper berries imported from Italy. We don't grind or crush them, they are steeped whole for the best consistency and flavor.*

# DSP or DNF?

If you're looking at starting a distillery—or have one already—you know what DSP stands for: Distilled Spirits Plant. It's the term assigned to our business(es) by the federal government and one we see on far too many forms. DNF is a phrase used in sports and racing and is one that most distillers don't want to hear or think about: Did Not Finish. Sure, finishing may have a handful of definitions whether your goals are to grow big and sell to a larger company, be a local tourist hot spot until you retire, or possibly just fund your retirement by doing this as a hobby. No matter what your long-term goals and outlook are, the important part is to have them. It can be so easy to get caught up in the magic and sheer mountain of things to do to get your doors open, but a lack of long-term vision and clarity has unfortunately caused a few DNFs in our industry over the years. This will likely increase as we see more saturation in the market with new distilleries popping up every day.

I use the term DNF as my descriptor purposefully—not just because it has a nice balance with the term DSP, but because I grew up a gearhead. Let me explain. DNF is thrown around a lot in racing—whether it be cars, bikes, boats etc. Just about everyone sets out to start a race with not just the intention of completing it but winning. We all tend to look at the end goal and sometimes forget about all the thick stuff in the middle. When I turned fifteen—the earliest legal point at which one can acquire a driving permit—I did just that. If you know me personally then you'll know I'm not the most patient person, at least on things that I find exciting. I won't be lining up to request an IRS audit early, but I did receive my SCUBA certification on the day I turned twelve (also the earliest legal age for that) and one of the greatest pet peeves of my life is missing the movie previews and getting a crappy seat at the cinema because we arrived late.

When I got my permit (my golden ticket if you will) I started a calendar to count down the days remaining until I could get my full driver license. My wife did the same. We'd compare the amount of days remaining, crossing them off one by one until we could each be free to roam around on four wheels. This was right before we started dating, as her father would not allow her to officially date until sixteen, so I had two things to look forward to. Our family had a Toyota 4Runner with a V8, blue, and I kept a set of white fuzzy dice in the center console that I'd pull out and hang from the rear-view mirror when I got my chance to drive. If you're already forming a mental picture of a ridiculous high school student who thinks he's cool, believe me, it's even worse that you are imagining. This was the family car however, and I was assured that if I continued busting my balls rowing on one of Seattle's crew teams, I'd get to have a car of my own to drive myself there.

I've still only had one speeding ticket and that was when I was sixteen. Shortly after I had saved some money and bought a radar detector, paying cash so it wouldn't be flagged on a bank statement subject to prying eyes. My mother brought this story up the other day—I had completely forgotten about it—and it makes me smile as I see my own kids starting to get crafty with things. I hid the radar detector in the center console, removing it after each drive so as to not get caught with it mounted to the windshield. Several weeks later my mother was driving with my older brother and the sun caught an edge of the windshield, highlighting two perfectly round circles in the center that looked like surprised eyes. Squinting, she said to my brother, "Now what on earth could that be from? It doesn't look natural." My brother Matt looks, takes about two seconds to think about it, then confidently says, "Those look like suction cup marks. Does AJ have one of those police radar detectors?". Oh, boy. This next part, I think, perfectly portrays a teenage boy's brain when confronted with a potential problem. "Be honest with me AJ, do you have a radar detector?" my mother asked. I was caught off guard—her very tactic, I have no doubt—and locked eyes with my mother, letting several seconds go by before answering, ever so slowly, *"Why?"*

You should always be honest with your parents, but that doesn't mean divulging every possible detail at any point in time. Yes, I owned up to the radar, and I can't honestly remember if I was allowed to keep it or not, but I can raise my hand and say I haven't gotten a speeding ticket since. Having my own car was a big deal, but I had to stay in sports which required a commute after school to qualify as "needing" a car. The same went for a cell phone.

I'm not sure if my parents were aware of how well that ploy worked to keep me in a sports program that broke my back on a daily basis (at least, that's how I viewed my time rowing), but it was damn effective. Of course, I now find myself bartering snacks to my own kids in trade for menial tasks, so perhaps it's written into the parenting DNA. Being the car-obsessed person that I was back then (and still am), I started the research process based on budget, reliability, looks, and power. But in the exact opposite order. What concluded my search was a bright red, I mean *bright* red, Mitsubishi Eclipse with some custom body work and an exhaust system. It also had to have a manual transmission: that was non-negotiable.

I should note, however, that my experience with a stick shift up until that point was nearly burning the clutch out on our church Bible study leader's VW and several driving lessons around our block with my father in our 1935 Ford. It had three speeds; first gear got you to about six mph, second gear was the sweet spot but you had to hold the shifter (also a die, but not fuzzy) to keep it from popping out, and third gear just meant you were going uncomfortably fast in a large old car with no power steering and bicycle-strength brakes. If you're familiar with automotive engineering, I should also point out that old cars like that had no synchros, meaning you had to either double-clutch perfectly or suffer the sound of grinding into each gear change. The Ford was apples and oranges to how the little Mitsubishi drove, and the day my mother drove me out to pick it up I had only had a handful of lessons in the Ford on our flat, 25-mph neighborhood road.

Driving away after purchasing the Red Dragon (I can't begin to imagine what was going through my mother's head following behind her youngest son in his first bright-red sports coupe) was comically entertaining. Starting from a stop required dumping the clutch, resulting in a long chirp of tire smoke from the front followed by a chassis-rattling judder while I held onto the steering wheel for dear life. I would be avoiding as many hills as possible for the next few weeks in order to save the tread on my tires and the cars behind me. Not four blocks from the man's house where I purchased the car was a long four-lane hill and as I swung around the corner going a good clip over the speed limit, I spied a local sheriff parked alongside the road. The expression on my face went from gleeful to terrified in a mere moment—undoubtedly exaggerated as teenage emotions often are—and to this day I think it was that reaction that might have saved me a ticket as I'm sure it brought the sheriff as much satisfaction as it brought me fear. Each shift brought as many cringeworthy grinding noises as our old Ford, the difference being that this transmission had synchros and it was not a natural noise.

Where am I going with all this? Buying that first car was a lot like starting a business. Yes, you can plan all you want. Yes, you can have the passion to figure out how to drive it (eventually). And yes, you can envision the finish line and whatever that means to you. But I'll be damned if you aren't going to grind a few gears and get some tickets along the way, radar detector or not. I did eventually put that car in a ditch eleven months later, fulfilling the prophecy foretold by my parents that everyone has an accident within their first year of driving. I blame the bald tires, which I now realize I was responsible for in the first place. Ka is a wheel my friends (Stephen King fans, you'll know what I'm getting at). I've been told more than half of new businesses fail within the first year—crash, if you will—and I believe it. It's important to have the passion to get going and to have a vision of the finish line, but don't forget about the stuff in the middle. Most of day-to-day business is that drive home, trying to find gears, endlessly buying gas, and having freedom of movement but not always knowing where to go.

## So, Why Gin?

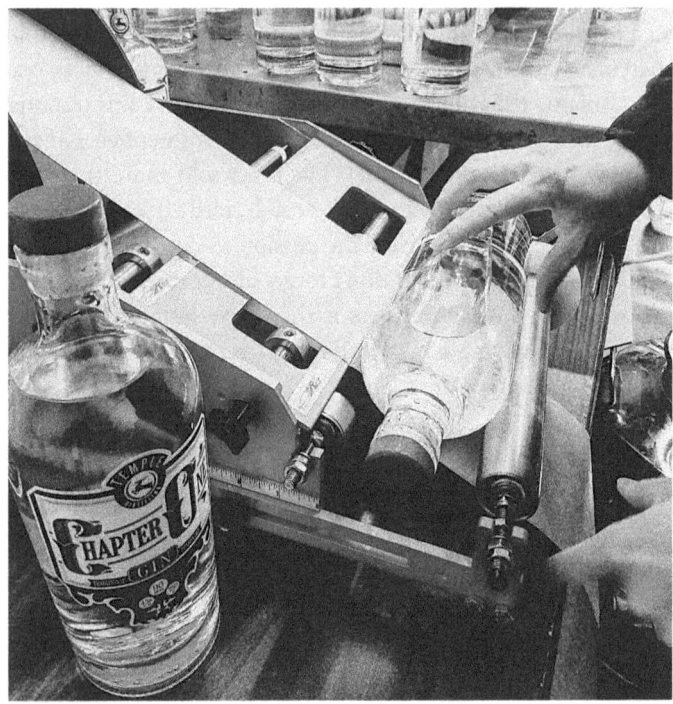

*The label machine we use to hand apply our labels, it's necessary because of the taper on our glass bottles. It may be a bottleneck (no pun intended) in our bottling line, but allows us great quality control on our gins as it serves as a time to inspect each bottle as it passes through.*

# You're Running a Plant

My first piece of advice to not put your business in a ditch? Pay attention to the last letter of DSP: *plant*. It sounds a bit clinical but at the end of the day we are all running manufacturing plants. As a manufacturer, it is crucial to focus on your business operations and marketability as much as on things like the taste of your final products. Taste is paramount to having a spirit succeed in the market, but that's just the thing—it's a market and needs to be treated as such. People can't crack open your bottles in the grocery store to try your gin before making a purchase. You're going to end up on a shelf next to fourteen of your closest competitors, so how do you stack up? If we forget marketing and just hope that people will *know* your gin tastes good, that shelf won't move much product. Next, you get bumped, and a year later when you've finally honed in on a successful marketing strategy, that store might not want you back based on poor past sales numbers.

Let's focus on business operations first, since they are the most tangible and usually the easiest issues to address when first getting started.

## Buy in bulk when you can

This not only nets you a lower cost per unit (whether it be bottles or botanicals) but also ensures consistency. You could find a supplier backlogged and suddenly you need bottles to fill an order. Not only do you have to pay a premium to get things rushed through, you could risk losing hard-fought shelf space to a competing distributor that sees an opportunity to swoop in. Botanicals may change based on the season, so buying enough to cover a year's worth of batches will ensure the same flavor profile upon re-orders.

A good example of this is an issue we had with our angelica root. This is a somewhat common gin botanical, and one that we use enough of that it is paramount to our taste profile. When we got started, I ordered a somewhat large bag, knowing that we would be doing a lot of testing, dumping batches, etc. Countless months of recipe development and we had settled on our final blend, which happened to call for 75 grams of angelica root. Fast forward several batches and we needed to order more. I pick up the phone and call our importer on the East Coast, order another 10-pound bag, and it shows up looking like landscaping bark rather than the delicate straw-yellow shaved root we had been using. I figured they had just switched suppliers, so I ordered 4 oz. sample bags from five or six other spice companies to see whose was the closest to our original ingredient. The following week became very interesting as each day a new sample showed up at my door, and each time I opened the box I was left staring, bewildered, at the same ugly landscaping bark! After talking to several suppliers in person and showing them pictures of our old angelica, it was determined that no one knew what the hell I was talking about and had only seen it look like the "new" stuff.

The closest explanation that I could conjure up is that the angelica we originally received was old—I mean a few years old—and boy were they probably happy to have us order their last 10 lb. bag of it! So, what did I do? Distill my friends, distill. I went back to chapter one (cough, cough) and ran tabletop distillations of each and every sample I was sent. I kept the neutral spirit volume the same each time, the run time and temperature dead on, and then tasted and compared. It's the *same* ingredient—despite its bark-like appearance—but due to the size and shape of the new roots we knew we would have to make an adjustment. The end result? We just had to dial our recipe back from 75 grams to 70 grams, end of story. Had we bought 100 pounds of it from the start we wouldn't have run into this issue—at least not for a few years—but if you can't afford to buy in mass quantities the next best thing is to know how to adapt when you get a curve ball like this.

### Always say yes

This sounds like it's straight out of a life insurance salesman training manual from 1963, but it still rings true. I've overheard complaints these past few years by retailers, bars, and distributors about the "fragility" of craft distillers and their concerns about their ability to get inventory when they need it, or having a distillery changing its mind on a key recipe and re-branding a product halfway through the year. It might sound great in a marketing press release to say that you sold out of something, or have "improved" your award-winning liqueur, but in reality there are ten other independent brands just waiting to snag your shelf spot. Real estate on a store shelf is finite. Some of the top cocktail bars in your city might only have an eight-foot, two-tier back bar with space for forty bottles. When a bar works with six distributors, each with fifty or more brands in their book, you can imagine that the competition for that space is often fierce.

We leased a warehouse last October—one that we don't need. *Yet*. Our main production warehouse is roughly 800 square feet and we've spent the last three years playing Tetris with pallets, cooling tanks, etc. trying to get everything to fit while still maintaining a functional workflow for bottling and other work. The problem we anticipated had to do with expansion into other states. Most orders will be sent out on a pallet, and even if it isn't full size, it still takes up the same large footprint on the warehouse floor. We have four gins and a limoncello in two sizes, so six total products that could be ordered at any given time.

This left us with two options: bottle on-demand when we see an order come in or figure out a way to store ready-to-go bottled product to just palletize and ship immediately. The latter we simply couldn't do in an 800-square-foot area; there isn't room to turn around a forklift to stack pallets even if we wanted to. The problem with bottling on-demand, however, is the logistical nightmare of six different products that all share the same bottling equipment. We're used to batch bottling, meaning we'll fill 400 bottles of Navy Strength gin, clean the lines and filter and then switch over to Woodcut Woodcut, our barrel rested gin, for 600 bottles. This method is much more efficient when you factor in the time to change bottling lines, the labeler, boxes, etc.

How do you do this in such a small space? Simple answer: you can't. We either risk delaying wholesale orders by weeks at a time or we pony up and get more space so that when those orders come in, we can ship them out two days later. When customers purchase something, they're used to getting it as soon as possible. If you get some lucrative orders that are then taking a month or more to show up to your customer, they might just find themselves a different product. Sure, you could win them back down the road, but sometimes those relationships fizzle out and you won't see them ever reignite.

Our warehouse situation was also unique because it was the warehouse right next door to us that became available. Convenience aside, there are several regulations at the federal level as well as state and city codes that may restrict where a second site may be established for a distillery. As a new business you should always be looking to expand—in this industry you tend to be either growing or shrinking—so never rule out the need for more space. If you can't find a space within a certain distance, however, you may be forced to apply for a whole new license which can take upwards of a year and a lot of time and investment. That's why we were so enamored with the girl next door. Not only can you not get any closer, it shares the same address (just a different unit number). All we had to do was revise our TTB permit, send a copy to the state, and we were in business. It took three days. So, although we aren't packing it to the brim (yet), the extra cost now is actually less than it would be to find a different space in a few years. Not to mention the logistics of moving heavy pallets and barrels via rental trucks or paying for ground shipping, additional security, and possibly two sets of city codes to keep track of.

So yes, don't be afraid to take calculated risks and say yes to the right opportunities. It's too easy to get stressed about your nonexistent cash flow and try to keep things as lean as possible, but go too lean and it can leave lasting scars on your business connections and potential opportunities down the road. That being said, we spent months coming to the decision about our expansion, looking over our books and forecasting sales to see if it would work. You might not get the chance to jump at every opportunity like that—that's just small business in a nutshell—but my point is to always keep an open mind and an awareness about your future positioning. And how to stay *lean* when you can?

## Use Ebay

Or Craigslist, or industry sites. Most of our equipment needs to be food grade and stainless. There are countless distilleries, wineries, and breweries that are expanding and growing and find themselves selling older, smaller equipment that they no longer have a use for or have outgrown. Most of this equipment is bulletproof and built to last longer than we'll be around, so go hunt for some deals. You'd be surprised at what is out there. You may find yourself buying from someone who used a piece of equipment directly and sometimes their advice can be just as valuable as the deal you're getting.

The lower your startup costs, the more cushion you have when the inevitable waves of business come rolling through. This is much easier than trying to control your variable costs when you get started. The more cash you have left over after your equipment purchases, the better prepared you will be for the inevitable changes in your variable costs like bottle and raw ingredient price fluctuations. I keep a list of equipment we either need or want in the near future, and I probably spend at least twenty minutes a day browsing Ebay for items on that list. It may seem repetitive, but one day I'll open a search and find that $900 transfer pump I've been wanting is available for $200. Suddenly the two production hours per week that upgrade will save me makes the purchase a worthy expenditure. Over a two-month period for example, $200 will have translated into 16 hours of additional productivity. While I'd like to say that time would then be spent playing three rounds of golf, it will inevitably be more valuable for sales calls and marketing work. I would have looked at the original price of $900 as $450/month over that time, which is considerable. But $100/month for the same thing? You get the idea.

### Have a plan for pricing and distribution

Some states only allow you to sell to the liquor control board so they can distribute and sell out of their own stores—and out of your own tasting room. Many states, however, are "open," meaning there is still government involvement but you can self-distribute or sign with one of several distributors in that state. We all know that added middlemen cut into profits, but at some point it becomes a necessary evil for many suppliers. I touch on distribution later in the book, but the takeaway in this section is to have a *tiered pricing plan* in place if you are starting out with self-distribution. You'll want to set your shelf price, then work backwards roughly 30–40% to get to your wholesale price. Your margins should be great at this price point, but keep in mind that your cost will have to be another 30–40% lower when you start working with a distributor. It's all too tempting to get greedy, knowing that you have no middleman, and undercut some of the larger distributed brands to land a bunch of shelf placements. Does it work? Yes, I see it all the time, in fact.

A few months ago, I was making a sales call at a local bar and we got to talking about their other local gins and how we compared on taste and price points, etc. I was familiar with the other local brands, and it's often pointless to compare pricing with the big brands because of their anchoring schemes. Importers and big distributors don't want anyone to know this (although most in the industry do): that all too often large gin and vodka brands get paired with other leading spirits like whiskey, and to get a desired whiskey a bar will end up ordering a pre-set "collection," with the price of the clear spirits being *much* lower than they legally should be. For the importer or portfolio-holder it creates volume for the gin and makes up the profit with the whiskey. It's an interesting shell game and a legal gray area, and it's one to be aware of if you think you'll come out of the gates swinging against a huge brand.

That said, I noticed that a local gin (who shall not be named) happened to be featured in several of the bar's cocktails, which considering the type of bar and other cocktail ingredients I found surprising as it didn't match up with the cost of the other drinks. The bar man-

## So, Why Gin?

ager told me (although he probably shouldn't have) that the distiller was selling his $30+ gin to the bar for $9. Well, it's sure working to get his brand in front of more people, but here's the problem: at some point that distillery will grow and need a distributor. If they sell to the distributor at $9, their new price to that bar is likely around $20 with tax, more than double what it was before. Does the bar double the cost of the drinks? No, they boot you out for something else. The consumer is now both confused by the sudden departure and wondering how you were featured in a $6 cocktail when your bottle at the store nears $40 with tax. Plan ahead, pick your retail price point, and work backwards two steps until you get to your theoretical distributor sell price. Then make sure you can support that margin, and if you continue to self-distribute, enjoy the double margins. Once you do eventually make a move to a distributor there will be no disruptions to your place in the market.

# Nuts & Bolts

So, you've made it this far, your palms are sweaty, and you've double-checked your bank account and life insurance policy just to be sure. You've figured, "What the hell, the kids will get along great without money for college," and nothing is going to stop you from opening up that gin distillery. What are we missing then? Nuts and bolts, the boring stuff. Ironically, I spend more time proofing gin (at least, wait time) than it takes to make it, and I'm always planning ahead for more equipment that we'll need. So, let's cover blending and equipment before you change your mind and run back to safety.

## Blending & Proofing

Blending and proofing a spirit is a seemingly simple process of adding water to alcohol, but it is one you don't want to rush through as federal requirements on accuracy are 0.5% ABV, or 1 proof variance. There are a lot of great resources out there for these calculations—the section in ADI's new book, *The Nano Distillery*, is a great example—but I wanted to offer a simple rundown.

What you'll need:

- Alcometers
- Temperature Gauge(s)
- RO (reverse osmosis) Water Machine
- Blending Software

You'll want certified alcometers that cover the range in proof of the spirits you'll be producing. If you have a big budget, I'd recommend purchasing a whole set from one to 200 proof. We opted to buy three that cover our spirits, and I use a cheaper, non-certified alcometer for our initial gauging.

The same concept applies to thermometers. You are required to have a certified one, but like the alcometers, they are expensive and since most are the mercury type, they aren't always the easiest to read. I honestly believe the accuracy of your naked eye somewhat negates the additional precision of those thermometers, meaning that while they are calibrated to 0.01 degree, the lines are very close together and not always easy to get a good read on from three inches away. The solution? Invest in a nice electronic probe-type thermometer, one that can be calibrated, and calibrate it with your certified thermometer. Keep a log and do this at regular intervals. Let me tell you it is much easier to take and log temperatures with the push of a button.

We use RO (reverse osmosis) water for blending because for gin, it is important to get a uniform integration of the oils present in the alcohol. RO water is essentially water with everything removed. It's not just filtered or distilled but completely scrubbed of anything that may be in it. Because it's been stripped of everything, it is physically looking for molecules to latch on to. I've even heard that drinking it straight can be unhealthy as it can bond to minerals in your body and remove them as you digest it. Don't worry, though, as once it's bonded with gin—a medically significant compound, as I've been assured and can attest to—it's perfectly safe for drinking. Small RO water makers can be found online at pretty reasonable prices. All you need is a water source and a 110v standard power outlet.

The process begins by taking a sample of your distillate and measuring the indicated alcohol strength and temperature. Every instrument is calibrated to 60 degrees—apparently that's the house thermostat setting for ethanol—so once you have those readings, you'll need to input them into your blending software. I would recommend ABS by Mountain Moonshine or AlcoDens. There are others, but those are the two I have used and liked. You can also use the TTB proofing tables, but they are only incremental to 1 degree of temperature (versus hundredths of a degree in the electronic software), so it is less preferable. I always recommend taking readings from the top of your tank (if you can reach it) as well as the bottom. Before the spirit has had time to rest and blend, you may find them slightly different. If you've blended well then chances are this isn't absolutely necessary. However, I find it offers a nice peace of mind.

You must now weigh your batch on a large floor scale. You cannot, I repeat, *cannot* use markings on your tank to guess the volume of the batch. The only way to achieve accuracy is by using weight, as weight combined with temperature and proof will always give you the correct volume.

Once you've entered the temperature, weight, and indicated proof of the spirit, the software will tell you the actual proof of the spirit, how many proof gallons of yield the batch made, and how much water (at 60 degrees F) to add to get to your target proof. My notation of the temperature is very important as most of us don't find our water coming out of the tap at exactly 60 degrees. Because of this, if the temperature is less—which it almost always is in our cold warehouse—then the indicated volume is technically denser and therefore the weight of water you were told to add is not 100% accurate. If you add all of the water indicated, you could risk over-proofing your spirit. Instead, I add about 85–90% of the indicated amount at a time. If it tells me 100 lbs. of water, I'll add 85 lbs. The mixture heats up when this happens, so I'll wait a few hours or a day, then repeat the above steps again, entering total weight and alcohol reading once it's settled. It may now tell you to add 13 lbs. Go ahead and add 10 lbs. Repeat. You get the idea, but you must be as accurate as possible and while this process can take longer than the actual distillation of the spirit, it is imperative you follow it.

The other option is to double-mortgage your house and buy a nice alcohol analyzer—all of the big guys have them—but when you're just getting started the methods above are my recommended course of action. And as always, take a quick measurement before putting the gin into your bottling line, just to make sure nothing has changed as it sat in the tank.

I should touch briefly on obscuration proofing, as we make a limoncello. It's a method I quite dislike, but there isn't a way around it unless you have expensive laboratory equipment or want to send every batch out for testing. Remember that lab still you purchased for running individual botanical distillates? You must use that to separate the sugar from your liqueur. Sugar affects buoyancy, therefore you cannot use your proofing alcometers as they wouldn't float in the correct spot, leading to an incorrect proof reading. Instead, you have to distill the mixture, leaving the sugars behind, then test the clear distillate that is produced instead. I say I hate this method because it leaves a sticky mess of burnt sugar in the lab still every time—that's how caramel is made, and it's not fun to get out of a small glass hole. You simply measure the volume of the liqueur you put in—let's say 500 ml.—and then measure the volume of your final distillate, which will be less. Say you've got 350 ml. of distillate and a sticky mess in the still. Now add 150 ml. of water to that distillate to get it back to the original volume. The alcohol will have all been distilled out, so this now "represents" the original liqueur sample—sans sugar—and can be measured accurately with your alcometers.

## Equipment

We use a 500-liter bain-marie-style kettle. We made this choice for a few reasons. The size was one, and I will have more to say about that later, but there were other functional considerations as well. For one, our space does not have gas for direct fire burners or a steam boiler, so we were limited on options from the start. Our primary reasoning, though, was that we planned to make dry gin in the traditional fashion by boiling the botanicals directly in the kettle. This process gives the oils more complete integration and thus delivers a more robust flavor on your palate. Additionally, with delicate botanicals present, we wanted the heat to be even and soft so as not to cause potential added stress from uneven heat and hot spots. Because of all this, the bain-marie made a lot of sense. We may not be making gallons of Bearnaise sauce—which is how I use my double boiler at home—but I put just as much care into our gins despite the slower heat up time of our setup.

Copper does a great job of cleaning up flavor and removing impurities, but you don't need it on every square inch of your still (although it does look pretty). We use a straight-through copper column and the rest of the still is stainless steel—it's less expensive and still lasts forever. There is a graph somewhere (and damned if I could find it to put in this book) that shows the relationship between the placement and use of copper on the sulfur content of the final distillate. Copper binds to sulfur—a byproduct of fermentation that does not impart a nice flavor—and leaves it behind in the still after distillation. The chart, which you have to now picture in your head, shows the efficiency of copper in multiple scenarios. If the still and condenser were all made of copper, if just the still was, if part of the still was, if there was only copper in the condenser, etc. It was interesting to see that every combination did indeed show different sulfur levels, but at some point using too much resulted in diminishing returns and you were just paying for the "bling" aspect. That said, sulfur presence tends to be a larger issue with whiskey, and the science and specifics I won't cover in a book about gin. I guess the point I'm trying to make is that each operation is different, making different spirits, and the selection and design of your still will impact all of that. Do your research, then consult other members of your distilling community, and talk to the manufacturers who make the stills. Use all of that knowledge, combine it with your vision of your spirits, and that should be enough to make a wise still selection. Don't worry, you've still got all of your recipes to figure out!

You'll need several tanks—also stainless steel—with lids. We use the "soft drink" approach and have a small, medium, and large tank at our disposal. The small tank (300 liters) collects the distillate and is on a wheeled pallet so we can move it around the distillery and onto the scale easily. Size this tank based on your kettle size. Ours is about ⅔ of the size of our initial charge volume. The medium tank (1000 liters) is where we do proofing. It still fits on the scale but has enough head room to take the proofing water and could also fit two batches if we need to do a back-to-back distillation. The large tank (2000 liters) is our attempt to emulate the big guys. It allows me to keep multiple batches of dry gin in rotation and blended together. Many botanicals can have seasonal swings that slightly affect flavor and the potential downfall of a truly small batch gin is customer concern that the bottle they purchased six months ago will taste different from the one they purchased today. This is the same reason we don't use batch and bottle numbers on our dry gin bottles. If you want to be someone's new go-to gin, you have to be consistent. Period.

Another thing to consider having on hand are several glass carboys, typically used for beer and wine, as they are handy for collecting heads and tails cuts, making small blends, etc. Stainless fusti tanks are great as well; they have handles for carrying them around and spouts should you want to bottle from them. Liquid can be very heavy, even in seemingly small quantities, so for larger tanks that don't have handles you need a game plan. For moving liquid between tanks and to your bottling equipment, you'll need a good pump or two. Because alcohol is flammable, they must be explosion proof. This is typically an expensive or non-existent option on electric pumps, so I'd recommend looking into pneumatic pumps. Invest in a decent air compressor and get a small pump for single-barrel transfers and a large pump for transferring between tanks, cleaning the still, etc. All the seals need to be food grade, so look for ones labeled "chemical pump" or "NSF." The same goes for hoses: They need to be both food grade and rated to handle high-proof spirits. Search "beverage hose" and other similar terms. I happened to find some bulk hose that I then cut and made fittings for. It saved us about 30% over a hose purchased from a distillery supplier, and it's made by Goodyear, so I figure if their tires can get me to work then their hoses should do a fine job as well.

The beauty of this business—much like the beauty of gin more broadly—is there are no two alike. Your space, budget, and vision will determine your specific equipment setup and how you approach making your booze. Consult your safety officials, talk to other distillers and producers, and budget an extra 25% on top for stainless fittings. Seriously, they aren't cheap, and you will always underestimate how many you need. Always.

## Get Comfortable with Marketing

Speaking of the market, let's talk about marketing. A word that either strikes fear or invokes images of bright neon dollar signs in one's head when uttered. Yes, most marketing requires money and creativity. Some businesses have one, the other, or both (but hopefully not *neither*). Every business is different, so I'll be making my suggestions in the broadest way possible. The reality of marketing is that you'll inevitably learn as you go regardless of where you started out. And, like us, you will probably look back on some ridiculous things you thought were passable at the time. Honestly, you should see our first label renditions, done in Microsoft Paint no less. Not even Pappy would sell in a bottle that looked like that!

## Visual Branding

Let's talk labels and packaging first. As distillers we can easily find ourselves focused 100% on what's in the bottle—what people will taste when given the opportunity. Here's the thing: *we have to get that bottle open*. If you're the one pouring it (in your tasting room) then that's taken care of. If it's sitting on a store shelf or on the back bar at your local cocktail spot, then it's another matter entirely. As our broker in Idaho loves to say, "we have to get liquid to lips."

When in the last stages of closing on a warehouse space and starting the mountain of federal paperwork to get our DSP off the ground, my wife and I thought (quite naively) that we could design our own labels. We had our brand name picked out for our flagship gin, we had some general ideas of the feel we wanted to achieve, and we had some design programs on our computer. As I mentioned earlier, I look back now at some of our first renderings and cringe at what we thought might be acceptable in the marketplace. If we were good at package design, we would have been opening a design business, not a distillery.

If there is one big idea that I had to learn working in management for ten years prior to this venture, it is to know when to *delegate*. No one is perfect at everything; we all have certain skills and passions that make us who we are. That may sound like a quote for a motivational poster, but it's the plain, hard truth. There are two main roadblocks that prevent someone from delegating: control and money. The first is hard to overcome for certain personality types—I know because I'm one of them. I tend not to trust anyone to do anything right, bittered by years of witnessing this firsthand in this interesting little place we call planet Earth. Diversity is wonderful but if you want something to reflect *you*, the answer is usually that only you can do it. However, hiring someone to do design work doesn't mean that you have to relinquish 100% of your control. If you find a good designer, they will ask you how involved you want to be in the process, so don't worry, you aren't completely giving up control.

For us, salvation came from a man named Scott (that's not a bad movie title either; maybe I'll file that one away for later). Jamie and I had landed on a white, square label, our logo the depiction of the letter "T" in a big, bright-red font. We had some black and white pictures from our trip to England the year before and a basic border of some kind. It was awful. I was ready to go to one of those websites that tricks college kids into pseudo-plagiarism to have them render me a label that looked at least somewhat presentable for our first release. Then came a call from Scott. Now, I don't normally answer unknown calls—I probably let this one go to voice-mail the first time—and I definitely have a bee in my bonnet about sales cold calls. I used to have to do them at the auto shop and I hated it. I found myself wanting to apologize the whole time for interrupting

## So, Why Gin?

someone's day and privacy by calling them on their cell phone to announce a "special" that was supposedly in their best interest to take advantage of. Let me tell you, being yelled at is no fun and is another reason I left that industry. I've never been yelled at for my gin or had blame placed on me for someone else's stupid mistakes, so I'm quite content right here, thank you very much.

Back to Scott. He found our number on a list of newly issued DSPs in the state. He was a local label designer who had worked with several beer companies and was looking for more work. Instead of grumbling about the fact my cell phone number can be found so easily online, I listened to the message and called him back. "Oh my God, please help us, I just hope you aren't $20,000." That was pretty much what I remember going through my head at the time, and yes, he did, and no, he wasn't.

Fresh Bread Design is the name of his company, and I like fresh bread. Especially with a cold piece of salted butter, and maybe some young Italian olive oil. And fig balsamic. Sometimes a dab of chili oil. Have you had it with a thinly sliced, rare-cooked tenderloin and some horseradish sauce? Or toasted and smothered in button mushrooms cooked in cream, garlic, and parmesan? This was where we were at—we had a product and some glass picked out to put it in, a vessel as you will. Bread is often a vessel, and we were all over the place trying to figure out what should be on it, what garnishes to use, and so on. You know the feeling when you're overwhelmed and panicking, yet someone asks you what you have on your to-do list and you can't seem to name any one specific thing? This was us at this moment in time. Scott came in, showed us some of his past work—which was stellar—and talked pricing. Everything he said meshed well with what we were thinking and hoping.

The next step was to figure out how the whole process worked. How do you tell someone to do your branding if you don't know what your branding is supposed to be? We were told there are several levels, ranging from "We have an idea and just want you to make it look prettier" to "We literally have nothing but some keywords and some kickass gin, please help." You can guess what camp we were in. We made a down payment and let him get to work. He took our theme and idea of wanting to be bold but traditional at the same time and came back with four directions to go. We then picked one, fleshed it out into a logo, made several revisions and called it good. Then we did the same with the labels—he allowed us to be as involved or uninvolved as we wanted to be. It was glorious.

The second hurdle of marketing, money, is sometimes an unavoidable roadblock. Unless you have a lot of it. I believe the saying goes, "The only way to make a small fortune in the drinks business is to start with a large one." What I will say on the subject is that paying someone else who has a special skill like design or equipment fabrication is an investment. Meaning it will pay off. "But AJ, don't some investments lose value or incur a lot of risk?" Yes. A simple answer, but one that also applies to everything else in business. If we were 100% risk-averse, we wouldn't be in business in the first place. In our case, having a professional design our labels and packaging netted us retail placements right off the bat. Why? Because unfortunately people *do* judge books by their covers, so we made sure our covers looked good on the shelf.

Sure, writing those first checks hurt, but we saw income from it a few months down the road as well as numerous, invaluable connections. My first writing gig that wasn't just recreational writing? That came from Scott's good friend who worked at a local newspaper and wanted guest writers for the wine, beer, and spirits section. Okay, that does sound a bit "recreational," but there were deadlines involved to go to print, so let's call it somewhere in between. You want a "free" brand ambassador? Just foster those relationships with your vendors and as they talk in industry circles your brand will stay relevant.

## What's *Not* In The Bottle

You'll also need to think about glass, corks, labels, tamper seals, boxes, shelf talkers, hang tags, sell sheets, and merchandise. Need a drink yet? There are countless combinations and directions you can take with the aforementioned items and while you should spend time considering all of them, try not to panic. There are tremendous resources for finding vendors who handle all of these components. Try consulting groups like the American Distilling Institute and local distillery guild chapters for a list of their associate members and sponsors. Manufacturers have been sprouting like weeds in the past few years and it's a competitive marketplace. What does that mean for you? It means they want your business and will gladly send you a myriad of samples. Get as many samples as you can, visit your local stores to compare with your competition, and keep hunting until you find the combination that fits your vision and the spirit that will be going into the bottle.

Marketing materials like shelf talkers and hang tags will either be up to you or your designer, but they should be consistent when paired with your bottle on a shelf. Don't use too many words and strive to keep things simple. You have someone's initial attention for all of about two seconds, and if you succeed in gaining their attention, then you have about five to ten seconds after that to get your entire message across. Personally, as a writer this was one of the hardest things for me to get right when designing our marketing material. My wife could see—from across the room no less—that my 2"x2" shelf talker had too much content on it (almost two paragraphs). You'd need a microscope to read it—an accessory I don't see available in most liquor stores unfortunately. Go lean whenever possible; it just works better.

## Sales Materials, Social Media, and Ads

Apart from packaging, most of your marketing efforts will be directed at developing sales materials and direct advertising. Sales materials wholly depend on your specific products and vision. Your designer may be able to do them, or you can tackle them yourself. Collect as many handouts and fliers from other distilleries and distributors as you can and study them to learn what is floating around in the market. Our early pricing sheets were utterly embarrassing, but we were working with what we had. Instead of paying to have them designed—budget was tight—I paid to have some professional photos taken of our bottles in a neutral background. With those files I was able to build some nice marketing material at a fraction of the cost it would have been using a third-party firm. Again, if it's not your strong suit, know when to delegate.

Advertising is its own beast—a beast with many heads—and it's up to you to figure out which ones to see through and which ones to lop off. We never saw a great response from print advertising, especially considering it tends to be one of the most expensive channels out there. If you're placed in or near a tourist destination it may serve you better. I believe print ads are most effective at driving traffic to a tasting room or some other tangible location. If you are simply making people aware of your brand and their local bars don't yet carry you, it's unlikely you'll see an increase in sales volume as a result. Know your audience and cater to them through their preferred channels. Facebook has worked very well for us, Instagram has given us an avenue for more stylized marketing and a surprising overseas interest, and direct email newsletters have also allowed us to advertise new releases and bars that feature our cocktails directly to our existing customers. If you have awards, go ahead and flaunt them. If there is an account that you think might be leaning towards bringing you on in a large fashion, tell your customers to go ask for your gin at that bar.

We're a family run operation. Just yesterday I posted a story to our Instagram feed, a video of my three-year-old son, Thomas, tossing a two-pound bag of juniper berries into our still and loudly exclaiming that we're "making *gin*!" I love stuff like that, and other people do, too. The trick here is knowing when to share more personal things like that video and when to keep it strictly business. A seminar I attended once touched on this, and their proposal was an 80/20 rule—80% business, 20% personal. I like that ratio, and I'd recommend using it as a baseline while realizing that your particular image and identity may call for more or less than that.

For the love of God don't make your personal Facebook page the official page for your distillery, but please also don't describe yourself on your web page like you're pitching to investors either. There's one distillery website that, on their About Us page, has three of the most boring paragraphs I've ever read in my life. Something along the lines of: "Our company, XYZ Distilling Company Ltd, Inc, is poised to enter and grow in many lucrative overseas markets. We are taking in new investors. We plan to make fourteen different unique and groundbreaking products [they only had vodka last I checked] and we will be distributing these through many large channels. We have a warehouse. We have a fancy bottling machine. We are awesome and will makes tons of money." You get the picture. Does it make me want to order a martini with their vodka? No. Not that you'd ever catch me drinking a vodka martini unless there was literally nothing left in the world but vodka and ice, and then I'd still try and figure out how to make it into gin. However, if their page was solely comprised of pictures of their dirty home kitchen and awkward cocktails served in mason jars, I don't think I'd be seeking them out either. Balance—it's kind of important. Know your channels (or heads of the beast, if you will) and know when and what to send through each of them.

## Shoot for the Right Awards

Another important component of your marketing is listing awards. Awards serve as recognition that the claims your label makes are actually true. You'll notice that every time you open your inbox or mailbox there will be an invitation to submit your spirits to an international competition of some sort. There are literally hundreds of these—some respected and some completely unknown—so choosing where to spend your money becomes very important.

You'll hear some people mutter ideas that these tasting competitions are just cash cows and are rigged, but the truth is that, in most cases, you are getting a fair shake and often some constructive feedback as well. The more well-known a competition is, the more expensive it tends to be. This is a necessary escalation because if it were less expensive there would be so many brands entering that judging would be all but impossible. The other end of the spectrum is a local judging panel that will be less expensive and likely have fewer entries, giving you a higher chance of scoring well as a result of less competition. The downside is touting an *Oahu Island Local Small Batch Spirits Competition* gold medal to a potential distributor would likely result in an eye roll and no call back.

My advice is to pick competitions that are well known, that your peers and other legitimate competitors enter, and that present themselves in the market(s) you intend to target over the next few years. If you aren't winning the awards you think you deserve, try to be humble and take the advice of tasting notes you get back. Maybe your recipe does need a tweak or your ABV an adjustment. Maybe your skill is in another type of spirit. This advice can be hard to swallow—especially if you have your future already planned out—but just like learning how to delegate label and package design, it sometimes pays to seek outside help and listen to constructive criticism.

Sifting through competitions and evaluating their merit also applies to other marketing channels like tasting events, auction donations, samples to publications and reviewers, etc. I can't offer specific advice when it comes to these decisions because these are things you will just learn, plain and simple. We quickly learned that some events were a complete waste of time and that some—OK, many—sample requests were just folks looking for free booze. Money and time lost in this endeavor are simply costs of marketing and growth as far as I'm concerned. Oh, and once you donate to an auction, be prepared for bi-weekly emails from every other benefit or auction within ten zip codes of your location. Vultures they can be, under the guise of doing noble work. I'm sorry, but I can't just drop everything I'm doing to make sure the donors at your benefit for feral cats get some free booze. Be a good local citizen and business owner but make your choices with wise intent for what's best for your community as well as your own business.

# Some Folks You'll Want to Be Friendly With

I know, I know, that's already a lot to think about just in terms of making the spirit and presenting it to a customer, but now we need to talk about some of the external "partners" you'll need to work with in order to actually make money off of your spirits. Due to the legal structures surrounding the production and sale of alcohol in this country, you'll want to be on friendly terms with these folks.

## File with the TTB

Let's talk paperwork, specifically TTB application and trademark. Although it may be expensive, find a good law office to help you out, making sure it's one that specializes in beverage alcohol or has dealt successfully with the TTB in the past. When you decide to pull the trigger on this crazy business, you must first obtain a space before even starting the paperwork for your license. This means committing to a lease and handing over cash, not knowing when or even *if* you'll be approved. I looked at it this way: a lawyer is expensive, but so is rent on an empty building.

We opted for a middle ground approach, hiring a lawyer to review our TTB paperwork that we had prepared and correcting any errors before we submitted. We could have paid three times as much and had them do everything for us, but our approach allowed us to save money as well as have their advice and support. The result? Wait times were six months at the time and we received our permit in less than two. If you do the math, four months of rent was close to $8,000, and we paid our lawyers about half that to start producing earlier, so we were ahead already.

Trademarks are also vitally important—albeit expensive—but they will minimize your risk of facing a re-brand early on, which can be very costly or even fatal to a young business. Go ahead and Google your proposed business and product names and be aware that U.S. Trademark Class 32 and 33 cover most beverages, so it's not just spirit names you have to check for duplicates/similarities but also beer, wine, soda, etc. Your law office can certainly help with this as well; plan for a couple thousand dollars per trademark in the end and a sizable wait time.

## Distribution

The last order of business is distribution. Every state is set up differently, so this advice is highly provisional, but there are some common threads to cover. First, when you're newly opened and not widely known, it is unlikely you'll get any callbacks from distributors. If you do, tread carefully as they may be new and hungry themselves and might not be a good match for your long-term vision. This can bode well in certain situations, but in many cases, you'll get locked into a contract and eventually find yourself stuck in a position where your business is growing faster than your new, small distributor. This could hurt in a couple years when you are ready to move your brand out and have to face the consequences of breaking contract.

The reality is that bar managers don't want to talk to a different person for each of their eighty spirits on the back bar, and stores don't want to go to the trouble of setting up a new vendor who only has one or two SKUs. They prefer to deal with a handful of people who supply ten to twenty of their products, and those are all reps for distributors. We don't want to drive to three grocery stores to get ingredients for dinner; we want a one-stop shop. Sometimes I'll make a trip to another market to grab fresh Chanterelles for a bisque, but that's because that particular ingredient is worth it and a staple for my dinner plans. If you are working the market alone, you need to be that fresh seasonal mushroom—one that a bar or store manager will make the extra time for. This doesn't mean that you should never self-distribute. In fact, there are definitely upsides to that approach such as the personal bonds you'll make with key accounts, but be aware it is not the easiest option if your state happens to allow it.

If you reside in or are expanding to an alcohol control state, where the state government-run stores are the only ones selling spirits, you won't have a traditional distributor. They'll require a representative for your brand, but what you'll be looking for is a broker—and a good one. Brokerage fees are generally 5–10% of gross sales and cover their time for promoting your brand. Marketing materials and trade show staffing can be extra, along with various other expenses that they may incur. You need constant boots on the ground if you don't want your brand to go unnoticed, and those boots may also include people besides those contracted with the state. Brokers and brand ambassadors may just be your first "employees," but they won't always be working for just you, so you have to make yourself present to get traction in the market. Brokers in large markets like California will likely want monthly minimums upwards of $1,000, so I would not advise entering those until you have more brand strength to justify the cost. Once you sign a contract, you're often locked in for years, if not life, and breaking the contract is expensive. This contract cost can be covered by a new distributor if you have brand strength, but if your sales aren't great it may just fall on you. It can cause more trouble down the road to enter a market too early, acquire and subsequently lose shelf space, then later try to re-enter with a reputation of poor sales. Start small and start focused.

Remember that this process takes time. I swear the rule of measurement for distributors is in weeks and months. If you're told "we'll get back to you next week," just plan on having to bother them in three and finally getting a response in about two months' time. I'll only spend a few hours per week on this with the bulk of my remaining time focused on our local market. It's like setting out a deep halibut fishing line in an area not known for halibut, all the while we've already got four lines in the water around a school of salmon. We know we'll catch salmon—they are the local market and very accessible. But, if an 80-pound halibut happens to wander along the ocean floor and take a bite on our lone pole, we won't complain about that either.

We had some growing pains with our first distributor because of their size—not just the amount of sales reps they had but also the size of their spirits book. We initially thought a small book would be fabulous as we were the only gin they carried, but the result was almost the same as, if not worse than, self-distribution because our margins were less. Bars couldn't meet a delivery minimum unless they wanted to order a bunch of obscure spirits. The two-bottle order we *would* have seen with a larger distributor, along with a regular stock order, is now a canceled order with that smaller distributor. The other side of the coin is a huge distributor where you can get lost in a large book. The rep doesn't have time to go over two hundred spirits, so they just fill a regular order, and no one realizes you are there, wanting to butt in on the back bar. Large distributors work best if you have a lot of marketing money or brand ambassadors to throw behind them so that your booze stands out better in all the noise. There's no perfect answer unfortunately. Try to find a distributor who is established but not massive, who cares about craft and seems genuinely interested in your brand and not just the ten retail accounts you are bringing to them.

## So, Why Gin?

*Kicking off our first volume of our Co-Authored gin series, the bartender who won our cocktail competition formulated a list of interesting botanicals. We distilled them individually, and here we are blending and taking notes to see what flavors work well with each other.*

## Some Folks You'll Want to Be Friendly With

*My wife, Jamie, along with Thomas and Eli peeling lemons by hand for our limoncello. The smell of citrus and a maze of kids toys, pallets, and distilling equipment is what defines our life most days. We wouldn't have it any other way.*

## So, Why Gin?

*This is Marie, a bain marie still powered by waste vegetable oil and electricity. The smooth, even heat of the double boiler setup allows us to use botanicals in the kettle and not in a vapor basket, lending the full and signature flavor profiles of our gins.*

# Think Forward, Work Backwards

With some pen and paper items out of the way, let's talk about physical considerations for running an efficient DSP. *Start by working backwards but thinking years forward.* I should hope you've written a business plan if you are serious about starting a distillery, and one section of that plan should be sales projections. These are almost impossible to write accurately, however, unless you come from another distillery or distributor. Sales data is either closely guarded or available at high costs from large marketing firms and is usually from larger operations anyways, so the only useful metric with these might just be a growth percentage per year. That said, you'll put numbers down regardless and what you need to look closely at are those three- and five-year volume amounts. Now, ask yourself this question: "Is my planned equipment size enough to 'comfortably' produce this amount on a regular basis?" In case you wanted to know, we saw 70% growth each year for our first two years, like clockwork, but our starting volume wasn't huge. Feel free to use that number, but please don't write me any angry letters if your pineapple celery brandy doesn't net that kind of traction in the market.

With gin, scaling up batches can be a nightmare. You aren't just doubling a mash bill for a tank twice the size or adding three hours to a vodka distillation run for more volume. What you have to consider with botanicals is the extra time they will be in the hot still and how that affects the final spirit. You can't just double your juniper and orange peel when moving from 50 gallons to 100 gallons. Well, you could, but it would mean the orange peel was cooking in hot alcohol for an extra 4 hours and in turn may now taste stronger and with an added graham cracker note you weren't expecting. So, to adjust, you add 30% more orange peel instead of doubling it. Another run and you find it's not quite enough now. You see where I'm going with this? Try this on a larger scale and with 5–15 botanicals and you're looking at a lot of time and money wasted if you have to buy new equipment two years down the line and re-scale your production and recipes.

Buy the right size equipment to start, or at least to suffice for 4–5 years. Our still is capable of making 300–400 bottles of gin at a time. Were we selling that every day, every week, or even every month when we first started? Absolutely not! But we've had a consistent product and no supply issues in three years of business, and we aren't near capacity either. This is the *thinking forward* bit I mentioned, so now let's talk about working backwards.

You have a production number in mind to shoot for—one larger than you think you need. Now, work backwards from that number to your still, your processing and holding tanks, your MAQ (maximum allowable quantity) of high-proof bulk alcohol allowed in your warehouse (refer to fire codes and your local inspector), and your budget. Everything needs to be sized to match. To get to our fantasy production number we knew we needed at least a 100-gallon still kettle. We ended up choosing a 130-gallon unit because it had an operating capacity of 110 gallons. Why 110 and not 100 gallons? Simple math. The drums that our neutral spirit come in are a standard 55 gallons each. The alcohol needs to be diluted prior to maceration and distillation by adding water. We wanted to dilute it to around 50% ABV, so take a 55-gallon drum and add that same amount of water and what do you get? 55+55=110. To charge our still we simply pump an entire drum of neutral spirit, then fill that drum with water and pump that in as well. This simple math has saved us countless hours of measuring smaller amounts and it has ensured a quick turnaround of our bulk material by not having uneven quantities stored and a subsequent risk of exceeding our MAQ and falling into a higher hazardous designation.

After settling on our still size, it was on to sizing our holding and processing tanks accordingly. Everything else after that should fall into place—or at least provide enough of a reference point to make decisions on secondary equipment. Every operation is different but for us we've found a sweet spot what we have. We're producing in an 800 sq. ft. warehouse, so we needed the smallest equipment possible. However, we also wanted the capacity to produce far more than we needed for the first few years of business. Also remember that smaller stills will take a shorter amount of time on a distillation, so if your 500-gallon still takes 18 hours to run, you need someone there for an 18-hour shift. Let's be honest: that is a rough workday, one where you may never get to see sunlight! You may be better off running a 250-gallon still—or two if you need—for a 12-hour day instead and running them 30% more often to equal your production needs.

This circles back to my original point of focusing on the plant portion of your DSP, always keeping efficiency in mind when sizing and choosing equipment. You can't quite measure things like marketing and label design with *efficiency*; however, they need to be just as well thought out as the physical components. Their efficiency will show (hopefully) through sales. The point of this section was to touch on the corners of a starting plan, it's not a comprehensive guide by any means but should help get your mind in the right place. That is, unless you're now thinking of going back to a warm, safe job working for someone else. Despite the stress, working for yourself absolutely rocks, and I still wouldn't trade it for anything, DNF or not.

Now that the getting-off-the-ground bits are covered, I want to take you through a day in the life of a gin distiller and offer a glimpse into my crazy, pants-less life. Don't worry, it'll make sense in a minute. Maybe.

# Production Day

Why did we do this again? Is the coffee pot clean (enough) to use? Where are my pants?

All good questions, and all are the start of that crazy thing we call a Saturday in the life of a gin distiller. These thoughts are seemingly pulled out of the ether as the snooze button is pressed for a third time, circa 4:00 a.m. at the Temple household. Yes, it's still dark and yes, it's still raining outside. Not that it can rain *inside*; I've always found that to be a very unnecessary adverb. Hey, it's 4 a.m., remember? This is how my brain gets its morning start and why I rarely remember the process of showering and getting out the door. Something about having a routine lets your mind wander into useless alleyways and somehow keeps you sane at the same time.

I get dressed in the dark, my wife still sleeping and our two-month-old sprawled out next to her on the bed. On the opposite side from me of course, as I apparently wasn't born with the instincts not to roll over and smother the child. Women are amazing this way—somehow fully aware of the surrounding dangers of everything, even while asleep. I smile, give them both a kiss, and double-check the baby monitor next to me to make sure our two-year-old hasn't woken up early to set about destroying the little bit of sleep my wife is enjoying at the moment. I have the responsibility of the older boy—I believe mostly because his proclivity towards some major nighttime injury is far less and I'm useless once I've fallen asleep. I slept through a fire alarm as a child, if that tells you anything. Babies and gin, it makes the world go 'round, right?

Why the early start? It means that twelve hours have passed since dropping those beloved satchels of botanicals into a mixture of grain alcohol and water and it's time to get to work. My distillation day technically started the night before when I decided what time I wanted to get into work the next morning and rewound the clock 12 hours to measure out and toss our botanicals into the still. Some days it works best to get there early so that I can enjoy an evening with the boys at the end of the day. Other days Dad needs his sleep and I'll sacrifice an evening so I don't have to wake up at 4 a.m.

Step one: coffee. At my old day job (keyword here is *old*, meaning I've made the terribly important decision of distilling full time now), my boss gifted me a coffee maker that uses those fancy little pods. Being the cheap, cynical person that I am I was sure that it wouldn't get used as the cost per pod far exceeds using our espresso machine with raw beans. What I didn't realize is how damn *convenient* those little things are; being able to have readymade coffee in mere minutes feels like a matter of life and death at times. I sure love German engineering. Fast-forward twenty minutes and I've showered, found my pants, and have a travel mug full of hot caffeinated joy to haul to the distillery with me.

My commute is something of a point of envy to many of my colleagues. If you've been to the Seattle area recently you'll know what I'm talking about. There are about half a million too many people, who all have cars, who traverse down only two main freeways that are far too small but cannot expand any further (though they try) due to geographical constraints. Oh, and apparently no one knows how to drive anymore, either. Needless to say, I don't miss commuting long distance. At this hour of the morning, especially, I have the two-lane road to myself and a quick six-minute drive to the distillery. It's Saturday, so that means I need to put out our tasting room A-frame signs for the soon-to-be-awake world to see on their weekend jaunts about town. We found an affordable warehouse space, which was crucial to even being able to start this venture, but one of the downsides is no street signage. This means that those little signs are the lifeblood of our tasting room. We're told to put them way off to the side of the main road, but I happen to know that whoever it is in the city department that handles those sorts of things doesn't work on Saturdays, so good for us! Out on the corner sidewalk it goes, and thus begins another day.

On a side note, the "mystery" of our location actually got us a write-up in the *Seattle Times* likening us to a speakeasy. We aren't by any means, but that has to add 10% to our appeal regardless of our lack of bartenders wearing clothes that came from an industrial hipster catalog. We do, however, serve some mean gin and tonics, and I have a beard, so we're halfway there.

It's now 4:30, and the "clack!" of the breaker being thrown to turn on our still controller is painfully sharp in my head. I cringe every time, but you can't be slow and gentle with a large power breaker, so life moves on. Our still, Marie, is a bain-marie kettle that uses waste vegetable oil as the heating medium—essentially a huge double boiler—and the oil is heated with electric elements in the outer jacket. The electric elements are powered by the wall controller which has features to monitor vapor temperature, set alarms, etc. One large benefit of knowing your still inside and out is knowing how long the heat up cycle takes—in our case it is right around two hours. What's the benefit, you ask? It's called a futon, it's upstairs, and I could use another 45 minutes of rest before the sun comes up. Now, it's important to note that we have the column temperature alarm, ethanol detectors, floor leak alarms, etc., as proper safety precautions must always be used when working with alcohol. You never want to leave your still unattended, but you also can't be expected to stare at a cold still for several hours unblinking, either. Legal stuff out of the way, I happily climb those stairs and get a little shuteye, setting my alarm and dozing off.

I should also mention that it's freezing, so I'm opting to sleep in my clothes underneath about thirty blankets. When we had the still controller installed, it needed heavy, three-phase power. Luckily, our building had that already (side note: always have an inspector check if you need this in a space to lease; landlords do not always know what the hell that even is and may just say yes to get a new lease signed), but we only had one spot on our electrical panel to hook in: the warehouse heater. Yep, it was heat or gin, and we chose the gin. So, while the still works on warming the place up, I catch up on a little sleep.

**5:30 a.m.** I'm rested, the kettle is just starting to get a little warm, and my coffee stayed warm, too. I've not much of a morning person—if you can't already tell—so I decide to start the day with computer work. I never in my life realized just how much electronic communication, research, and involvement it took to run a business that makes a non-electronic product and sells it to brick-and-mortar locations. The first twenty minutes or so are spent cleaning out my various email inboxes. Eighty percent of them are junk, fifteen percent are actual important conversations with distributors and industry members, and maybe five percent are "decent" cold call emails from industry manufacturers and suppliers that I actually open to peruse the equipment and wares they have to offer. I have a system in place to handle all of these communications, and I usually like to hammer out the big inquiries first thing before I start getting distracted by some new alcohol pump that we don't need and can't afford.

# Production Day

Take this particular day: I've received a lovely email from the TTB (the Alcohol and Tobacco Tax and Trade Bureau), our governing body for all things distilled, that has the dreaded subtitle "Needs Correction" on a recent formula we submitted for a limited release gin. *Insert expletive here.* No matter how much time you spend back and forth with the TTB—or any of our regulating bodies for that matter—that is one thing that you can never claim to master. For every question there are three answers, all of them correct. Maybe. It depends on the day of the week and where we are in this particular lunar phase. I won't ramble any further on the subject so the next thing to do is find my login credentials for their online portal. After one attempt, I must now reset my password. Again. For the twelfth time this year. And it's only April. Here I go breaking my promise not to ramble, so let's keep going.

I come to find out that several of our ingredients require an advisory notice from the FDA, or Food and Drug Administration, which to go through official channels takes a minimum of two years. There is no way that can work with our release, so this information now prompts about 30–40 minutes of online research to find "ammunition" with which to equip the TTB so they will feel comfortable allowing our use of these ingredients without incurring any adverse responsibility on their end. One thing to remember is that no one, in any regulating body, wants to be accountable for any possible backfires and liability related to some kind of official ruling on a consumer product. What this means is that the gritty work has to be done by you, the distiller, in order to get things moving. After scouring through multiple trade publications, I've found a food additive ingredients manufacturer who happens to have a data sheet specifying allowable PPM, or parts per million, content of this particular ingredient in alcohol beverages—in this case it's the oil from the Shiso leaf. That done, I re-submit our formula with the required attachments and sit back with my fingers crossed for the next several days. That story works out well in the end by the way.

Distributor sales emails have all been answered next, meetings arranged if needed, and new marketing material sent out for review. Our marketing department? Oh, that would be me. Being that I run both our marketing and sales department, it's basically up to me to get traction in the market. Our new distributor is great, but they have two hundred other brands to tend to as well, so if you aren't pushing regularly you won't see regular sales. I always spend a few hours each week sleuthing through distributors in other states (and countries) and sending out emails to inquire about working together. One thing to keep in mind is that it takes months, sometimes years, to start working in new states because of how long distributors and state regulators take to get things done. Even if you don't think you can afford the travel and time to expand yet, at least start the process.

We're now about twenty minutes away from the still being warmed up so I meander my way out of my office and down the stairs. I love being able to see the column temperature on the still on a bright electric readout, but that will never compare to using my hands and really saying "hello" to the still as it warms up. Heat rises, so I start by lightly touching the kettle, which is now too warm to hold your hand on for more than a second or two. Next I run my hand up the copper column and feel the heat dissipation, knowing that the top is almost at full temp and we should be seeing vapor production very soon.

*6:30 a.m.* The *Beep! Beep! Beep!* of the column temperature alarm is music to my ears and it's time to make gin. Before wheeling over the main collection tank for this run, I set up a glass carboy with a funnel to catch the first of the distillate. This is a heads cut, but not in the traditional sense as it would apply to distilling whiskey and other spirits. Since our neutral base alcohol is pure ethanol, there is no need to make a cut based on other alcohol isotopes. Critical to the gin, however, are the botanical oils, and cuts should be made to achieve your desired flavor profile as well as limit (if desired) the amount of *louching* in gin, which is when the spirit clouds up in a cocktail or when added to ice. The oils that come over first tend to be the primary culprits and I have my recipes dialed in to remove certain amounts before collecting our gin to be bottled. The first cooling water tank is activated and within several minutes we are collecting those precious first drops of gin.

This is where I taste regularly, testing for taste itself as well as louching when I splash some water in my glass. For us and our recipe the changeover happens in roughly a half-gallon period of collection—meaning about 1/10th of our 5-gallon carboy as I'm watching it fill up with our heads cut. I save some of this distillate; after all is said and done, the proof is high enough to work well as a cleaning agent for various things around the distillery.

6:45 a.m. Heads cut taken, the large tank is now rolled into place and we are on our way for this production run. What to do now? If we have East Coast calls to make, it's about time to make them while the West Coast is just waking up for the day. Since the run has now "started," there isn't much maintenance needed on my end besides tasting the distillate every so often to make sure things are on track. We have to switch cooling water tanks twice throughout the day as they heat up, so I note in my head when those times should be and make sure to start checking them around those marks.

*7:00 a.m.* Our two-year-old is just waking up at home, and my wife starts pinging my phone with little "good morning" videos, which can either be cute or painfully hilarious depending on which side of the bed little Thomas woke up on today. Those videos make me miss him already, but I'm definitely one of the lucky few. Despite long days like today, I am right there with him most mornings as I no longer have a long commute and time clock to live by. Sounds great, but it does certainly come with its own stresses and drawbacks. Anyway, here I am, and once I've touched base with the family, it's back to the computer for a little while. The next hour is spent doing our monthly taxes and reports. We maintain several spreadsheets that track our inventory—how much we've bottled and moved in and out of the warehouse, sold to distributors and customers at events and in the tasting room, and how much (or little) money we've collected. I have to pore over these, along with my distillation production logs, in order to fill out all these forms. For the TTB, we have three monthly forms that track inventory, bottling, storage, and production. For our state, we have a form that tracks production as well as the different tiers of sales data, and then of course the excise and B&O tax forms for any small business or registered corporation. Oh, and quarterly tax reports, can't forget about those.

*8:00 a.m.* Forms done, copies printed and filed, and electronic copies uploaded to a backup cloud storage drive. Time to microwave a Chinese pork bun—to serve as a balanced breakfast—and get to work in the warehouse. Because we have no official street signage, we've been using Groupon to sell tour and tasting packages. This has proven to be a great "electronic sign" for us, but it also means I can't be leaving buckets and hoses all over the warehouse floor. I could, but that might hurt our reviews or, worse, hurt the reviewers themselves.

*8:45 a.m.* Cleaning done and I'm thinking, *Hey, we can actually fit another pallet somewhere!* Keep in mind we have roughly 800 square feet to work with and make five different products, so space is always much tighter than we'd like. I tell all of our tours that we are constantly playing a game of Tetris, and that is basically as accurate as it gets. There's a batch of Navy Strength gin in our proofing tank that needs another reading, so I collect some gin from the top and bottom of the tank and take readings on alcohol content and temperature with our gauging equipment. It's then back to the computer to input those readings and calculate how much water to add to get to our final proof of 114. It tells me 83 lbs. of water, so I go ahead and run our RO (reverse osmosis) water maker and add a little less than the indicated amount, mixing to blend it all together. The added water has raised the temperature and caused things to "wake up" in that tank, so I'll mix it and let it rest until later when I'll take another reading. Word of advice? Always add less than your instruments and programs tell you, unless you happen to have water that is at exactly 60 degrees Fahrenheit when blending. Work your way up to final proof; it can be a dance at times.

*9:30 a.m.* It's been three hours since I turned on the condenser water, and one of our three water tanks is now heating up. One of these days I'll have a pump for each tank—or better yet a glycol chiller—but until then I quickly switch off the water pump power, move the pump to the second tank full of cold water, and plug it back in. Presto! Condenser is cooling nicely again for another three hours.

*9:35 a.m.* Now tasting some cubeb and pepper notes coming from the still, so things are right on track. Since I'm there already I perform a quick equipment check, looking for leaks, odd smells, or anything else out of the ordinary. All is well, so now that I have a little over two hours until we open to the public, I decide to hammer out some bottling. Today it's limoncello, which we bottle straight out of the 13-gallon stainless fusti tanks we store it in after filtering and blending. It's a lot of work but at the same time quite convenient as we don't need to spend hours cleaning sugary liqueur from our normal bottling lines and I can bottle an entire batch myself in just a couple of hours. I grab handfuls of bottles from one of our pallets, blow out and sanitize, fill, and cork them, and then hand-apply the labels. The label machines do not like the shape of our limoncello bottles, so we figured that since we already hand-peel the lemons, we might as well keep the hands-on tradition going. Neck label is next, followed by numbering batch and bottle numbers with a pen, and finally the shrink wrap on top. The almighty white board on the warehouse wall is where I record how many were bottled before taping up cases, filling them, and putting them away. This later gets entered into one of many, many spreadsheets. Definitely learn how to use Excel if you're going to stay organized and in compliance.

*11:45 a.m.* Bottling complete—about ninety bottles in all—and I've only missed about twenty emails in that time. The tasting room opens in fifteen minutes, so it's time to make sure we have plenty of tasting glasses, some citrus and ice for cocktails, and check that things are clean and orderly throughout. Unlike wine, we don't have to dump sample bottles after each day, so I make sure we still have plenty of gin available for tasting flights and drinks. Music is now playing on the speakers, the heaters turned on—because it's still April in Washington State and the word "spring" hasn't quite taken it's hold yet—and ample inventory is laid out should our visitors want bottles to take home. Any additions to the tasting room or bottles opened for sampling are recorded on one of the many spreadsheets, and we can officially begin the day for the public.

*12:00 p.m.* We're open, and the next hour will either be spent replying to emails and calls or pouring samples for patrons who come in. I greet everyone cordially and go over our different tasting options, eager to start pouring and talking about gin and why we love it so much. If we're busy, this part of the day goes fast. Our tasting room location doesn't get much traffic, mostly because there isn't much around us. The city of Lynnwood has one brewery and no wineries or other distilleries. Not to say there aren't others within a reasonable driving distance, but unless you're hammering the advertising don't expect to see a massive amount of tasting room traffic if you aren't in a lucrative area. This was a trade-off for us—knowing we wanted to lean more heavily into wholesale and distribution versus spending all of our time running a tasting room. The margins are much better with retail—don't get me wrong—but you'll need employees sooner (added cost and headache) and you'll be spending too much time being there and not at accounts selling your spirits. The result is local popularity, but slow growth moving outside your market.

*1:00 p.m.* My lovely wife shows up with our kids. It's nap time, and Thomas and baby Eli both have cribs upstairs they are patiently waiting to occupy. It's great to see everyone; we have a few moments together for family time (if we don't have customers), and then put them down for sleep. This signals (usually) two hours of uninterrupted time for my wife and I to catch each other up on everything going on and trade off working in the tasting room. There's a ridiculously good Thai restaurant down the road from us, so if we don't have leftovers from the night before I'll pop down and grab us lunch. I'm a "five star" kind of person, so if I'm opting to go spicy I just hope I'm not too red in the face to serve newcomers or they might think I got into the gin tank too early. Before I go, it's time to switch over to our last cooling tank, same program as before.

*3:15 p.m.* Thomas is awake! We can hear the bleating over the baby monitor in the warehouse and one of us goes up to rescue him from his captivity, also trying to be quiet as Eli is still out and every moment of sleep is precious—probably for the kids, too, but mostly for our parental sanity. The tasting room closes at 5 p.m., so we determine if the kids and my wife stay until close or head out early and leave me to close up. With Thomas awake it greatly reduces the efficiency with which we can complete tasks, so our productivity naturally slows for these last few hours. I don't mind a little game or two of soccer in front of our bay door with my boy, but I do mind the "rearrange the tasting room bottles" game he so mischievously enjoys.

I find myself envisioning my boys growing up and saying that they were raised in a distillery and the kind of looks from other parents that story will garner. It's pretty badass if you ask me—they have an absolute ball playing and running around the warehouse space, and also respect the equipment and work that their mom and I do there. Just nineteen more years until Thomas can bring home his own bottle!

*3:30 p.m.* The gin is tasting great and juniper is starting to come through. It's one of the heaviest botanical oils and typically the last you'll taste during distillation, so I know we're getting close. Besides taste, I target 86 to 86.1 deg C in vapor temperature at the spot where our probe is placed in the still column, so now begins the dance of watching for those numbers and combining them with what my palate is saying to determine when to shut down the run.

*4:26 p.m.* We've reached it! The batch is done, so I switch to our "tails" collection tank and turn off the heat to the still. It's a ways off from cooling down, but this begins the shutdown process for the day.

*5:00 p.m.* The tasting room is officially closed. We've had 10 people in, sold 7 bottles and a T-shirt, and after tasting fees and tips collected a total of about $400, which we consider a pretty solid day. I walk to the street and pull in the signs, grab the mail, and head back to lock up. I'm exhausted—not physically, per se, but the mental fatigue of tending things for almost 13 hours takes its toll. I'll be honest, if it's looking like the still needs another 45 minutes of cool down time, I'll scavenge the last of that tonic bottle we opened for tasting and pour myself a nice G&T and watch some *Top Gear* on the TV we have upstairs.

*5:15 p.m.* The still has stopped dribbling out the tails and the condenser has been shut down, so no G&T today (at least here, but dammit if I don't have my mind set on a Woodcut Negroni at home. Maybe two.). Final checks are made on the equipment and it's time to bust out of here.

*5:30 p.m.* Arrive home. Kiss the wife, hug the kids, then find my mixer and some ice. Sometimes I go right for the fridge and am reprimanded for neglecting a welcome-home kiss, attempting to craft some excuse that doesn't match the bottle of vermouth in my hand and guilty look on my face. I find the couch, set my drink down, and warmly welcome my oldest to climb up so I can read him some of his many books. I like the short ones—not because I don't enjoy reading to him, but mostly because I don't want to spend twenty minutes answering questions about a saggy, baggy elephant and why he's so sad all the time. That poor elephant.

The rest of the night, as you can imagine, is winding down, and I'm one of those crazy people that does this by cooking. I mention to my wife I'd like to make some risotto and Scallops Provençal for dinner and as usual she rolls her eyes, asks if I'm sure after such a long day, and then says, "That sounds delicious". After two hours of cooking and a late dinner, it's reading or one of our Netflix shows and off to bed.

## So, Why Gin?

Tomorrow? Clean the still, bottle London Dry gin, two hours of account visits with our downtown Seattle distributor rep that will undoubtedly turn into a four-hour excursion after drinks and socializing, and finalizing our new bottle hang tags to be sent off for printing.

So, when we aren't making what's in the bottle, what does my day look like trying to sell everything else? Hint: it still starts with trying to find my pants.

# A Day of Many Hats

*7:00 a.m. Crash!* Blinding light, giggling, incoherent demands. It must be time to wake up, as Thomas has barged in on our peaceful sleep. Like the movie *Groundhog Day*, this is our life right now. Every. Morning. In his room there's an alarm clock that lights up at a preset time, and we've taken the Pavlovian approach to training Thomas, so he waits for his light to turn green to leave the bedroom and come wake us up in the morning. It's an absolute wonder of modern technology—with the exception of the 112% child energy thrown at us all at once each morning while Jamie and I are mid-REM cycle. It can be brutal at times, and this morning is no exception.

After more showering, pants-searching, and coffee, it's time to start another day.

*8:00 a.m.* Espresso number two is finding its way into my cup—bitter silky goodness that it is. The kids are downstairs running and crawling about, my wife is hurriedly trying to whip up breakfast for everyone, and here I sit at my computer. From a distance—in this case from the dining room table to the kitchen where Jamie is working on her semi-glare, and doing it quite well—it may seem like I'm being lazy. This is the (some might call unfair) routine, but many of our accounts do all their "work" in the morning because they open up for lunch service and once that happens they aren't taking sales calls.

## So, Why Gin?

The first hour or two of my morning is spent on the computer—reaching out to current and potential accounts, distributors, event coordinators, etc. I go into a sensory deprivation chamber of sorts, tuning out the incoherent demands of hot chocolate and movies, and focus on all the flagged emails in my inbox.

It's a tricky business, working a web of potential clients from a distance. In theory I should be physically in that neighborhood, knocking on doors and try to get tastings scheduled, but I've found working this part from home is more efficient. I spent a few days in market with one of our old distributor reps. We wandered from place to place with a rough plan and some names but only saw 20%, maybe less, of those buyers in person. Yes, it was fun grabbing drinks at different spots and talking spirits, but I'm there to sell our gin. Without appointments and a knowledge of when people are available, physical trips should be the last step since as a supplier you are typically there to close a sale, making use of previously established relationships.

***10:00 a.m.*** I've sent thirty emails, made a few calls, and sucked down two more cups of coffee. I've received a few responses for tastings today, so I start planning my attack on the city. The first tasting is at 2 p.m., leaving me a few hours to bust out some bottling at the distillery. We also have an event tonight that I have to load up and prepare for.

***10:30 a.m.*** Arrive at the distillery, fire up the air compressor, and take stock of the bottling equipment. I begin by gauging proof of our London Dry, just to double-check, and then hook the holding tank up to the filter that then feeds the bottling machine. I could do all of this with my eyes closed at this point, but then I recall the time I forgot to snap a line in correctly and received a face full of gin when I powered on the pump. That kind of activity should really be limited to people on spring break—although I smelled great the rest of that day (eat your heart out, Old Spice).

I spend the next two hours bottling gin by myself. It's tedious, but oh, so satisfying at the same time, and makes time go by quickly. Our bottler is gravity fed: I simply turn on a pump that fills the trough above, then insert bottles below and fill them until they reach a certain level. I pull the bottles off, cork them, and roll them onto our labeler. Two rolls with the hand applies the labels, the neck label goes on, and finally a shrink wrap on top using a heat gun to form it onto the neck.

*12:30 p.m.* I've filled about twenty cases of gin—one row of a full pallet—and am glad to have that inventory ready to fill orders. It's time for lunch, and because I don't make it into the city as often as I'd like, I search for what's around my tasting appointment to see if there is anything good. All the great restaurants seem to move to the city, so I relish any chance to try new things. I've been on a poke bowl kick and fresh tuna is like a drug to me, so I land on a perfect spot within walking distance of the bar.

*2:00 p.m.* After a very satisfying lunch, it's time for that tasting. There are two ways to approach tastings that I have found to be effective. The first is as straightforward "salesman" as you can get: go in there, tout the medals you've won, present sales figures and marketing materials, woo them with your competitive pricing, and push to close a sale. The second strategy is to play it *cool*. Ask questions about the bar and its history, casually pouring your gin samples and maybe sliding over a sales sheet at some point for the bar manager to glance at while you're engaging him or her.

## So, Why Gin?

I personally prefer the second method. You get to know that person better and since they might be accustomed to distributor reps running tastings, who almost always go with option #1, you are a refreshing change of pace and may just lock in the sale because of it.

Everyone has a different skill set and personality when it comes to sales, so take my outlook with a grain of salt. In my honest opinion the biggest game is confidence. I was so nervous that first year. We'd rarely get callbacks, and when we did, we made a huge deal about them in our minds. Our sales sheets were terrible, but at least the gin was good. Having not ever done this for a living, learning what is allowable and expected at tastings took some time.

Now, I simply just walk in with our bottles, some marketing material, and have a great time. You have to remember that you are the distiller; there's an extra cool factor that goes along with that, so use it to your advantage.

*4:00 p.m.* I know, it's two hours later, but the part I left out consisted of several more tastings just like the first one. In Seattle, most bars open up at 4 p.m., so the tasting window is effectively closed now that service has begun. I have an event to pour at around 7 p.m., so I've got time to kill and I'm thirsty. Evening hours when your accounts are open are a great time to visit, but don't try to make sales during that time. Simply being a patron—spending your money and ordering some of your own product at their bar—goes a long way. If you never see your accounts, and they don't see you, what's to stop them from switching to another kind of gin? Loyalty is a two-way street.

*6:00 p.m.* Event load-in. In the back of our Jeep we have six cases of gin, two roll-up posters, a hand truck, five hundred plastic tasting cups, a stack of medals, and some marketing material. Each event is different, but you find your setup routine pretty quickly. Find your table, check in and report your inventory, and get ready to pour.

Public events are a necessary evil. Well, that's not entirely true—it's not that people are evil, it's just that these events are often exhausting and the take-home isn't much. A certain percentage of folks are just there to get drunk, some were dragged by their significant others and don't even like spirits—this is especially true at "mixed" events that have beer and wine—and some will genuinely fall in love with your products and maybe buy a bottle. Looking back at our first couple of events, I'm embarrassed at the sheer amount of gin we brought, thinking we were going to sell a bottle to every person who purchased a ticket. Then the subsequent walk of shame, carting twenty cases back to the car at the end of the event four hours later…

Events are for showing face; actual sales tend to come second. If your local competitors are all there and you aren't, what does the public think about you? They *don't*—and that's why you show up. And then there are people who don't like gin (who are we kidding, they can't really be *people*, can they?).

I was pouring at a tasting event about a year after we opened and was approached by a woman who seemed to dart her way through the crowd to belly up to our table. Great! It was getting a bit awkward trying to somehow entice groups of people to our little station without seeming like a snake oil salesman. The lack of décor (and when I say lack, I mean we quite literally had just three bottles on the table with pour spouts, a sad little email sign-up form, and some business cards) was not helping. It probably wasn't the beard or that eager twinkle (not desperate, I told myself desperately) in my eye that drew her in but perhaps a subconscious mothering instinct, one that says,

## So, Why Gin?

*Go to the poor children, for they need comfort and attention.* This is when we cue the orchestra, the anticipation building for that first interaction and the start of a lifelong customer relationship.

"What spirits do you have?" she asked with great interest, her posture shifting forward and eyes intently examining our sparse expanse of wares.

"We make gin!" I exclaimed, perhaps a bit too bubbly for the situation at hand. The beard really didn't help this much, either.

You can probably guess what happened next, but for the sake of my story I should give it the ending it deserves. The word gin suddenly transformed itself into a four-letter word.

"Gin!" she exclaimed, and for one brief second, thinking I struck gold with a lifelong gin lover, my smile widened closer to my ears. "Auck!" was the word (or, rather, sound) that proceeded not a half-second later, roughly ten to twenty decibels louder this time. Her face, once bright and intent with the thirst for knowledge twisted into a hideous, disfigured snarl. You'd have thought I just told her that her steak was made with day-old roadkill instead of Wagyu beef!

The worst part was that after this outburst of disgust she remained standing before me for another five or ten seconds as if to ask what I planned to do about this unforgivable situation. Whatever I said next didn't get me thrown out—so at least I can say it wasn't as offensive as declaring myself a gin maker—but I remember suggesting to her she at least give it a try.

"There are no two gins exactly alike. Our gin has won awards. We have some tonic to water it down," and so on. The next part—and

I've seen it in kid's shows and cartoons but never from a living adult—she actually *harrumphs* and manages to march-stomp away without another word. If a grown person could have something akin to a muted temper tantrum, this was as close as I'd seen. I've heard with children that a thimble of whiskey works wonders. Perhaps her parents gave her gin instead, leading to a lifelong association between the two. Whatever the reason, she left a lasting impression not of sadness or anger but of ambition. How can I reach those people who are seemingly unreachable when it comes to this divisive and delicious spirit?

The answer is *persistence* and the acceptance that, well, you simply can't reach everyone. That statement may be contradictory as I read it back to myself, but so are people, so at least I understand my audience.

10:00 p.m. The event finally ends. My hands are sticky from grabbing our limoncello bottles, my feet hurt from standing on concrete for four hours, and my throat is sore from speaking the same prepared run-down of our gins repeatedly all evening. I load the leftovers into the car, wait about an hour to get a check cut—legally we have to get paid that night, whereas I'm sure most there would have preferred a check in the mail—and finally get on the road.

If it's just me, I head back home, hang with Jamie, and have a glass of wine and some Kraft Mac & Cheese (don't judge; comfort food rocks) and go to bed. Many events really necessitate two people, but we can't drag the kids along, so Grandma and Grampa often get them for the night. We find that we use most of our babysitting good graces for working, not having date nights like we should, so sometimes we just need that pre-midnight stop at the Roanoke Inn for a greasy burger and cold beer. Bliss.

# So, Why Gin?

A day of many hats indeed, but after making a few sales and some new gin converts at the tasting event, it's enough fuel to get up tomorrow to do the same thing.

The day after that? We'll do it all again.

Would I change anything? Absolutely not.

# Bitter Aftertaste?

Ah, Campari, how I love your bitter assertiveness bouncing off an earthy, sweet vermouth and bright, citrus-heavy gin. Negronis are one of my favorite, near-daily cocktails, and I think it's the bitterness that really draws me in. Much to my chagrin, I'm still trying to convince my wife to like them as much as I do, but you can't win every battle. Plus, making her a gin and tonic is easier and cheaper (although lately I've made headway using a splash of amaretto to sweeten the negroni a bit for her, a good tip when pulling people to the "dark side" of love for bitter drinks).

Is there bitterness associated with this business? Of course, there is. My advice? Learn to like it. Expect and enjoy it every day. The spirits business is tough. The big guys have truckloads of money in everything from marketing to lobbying in order to protect their interests. You won't get a paycheck as soon as you'd like to. In fact, you'll likely be riding out some home equity to finance things in-between (just ask me how I know). Not everyone is cut out to deal with the stress or complications that come with all of the hoops to jump through, but if you're passionate and have the talent to make good juice, you just might be alright.

Things often just take time to mature—barreled gin and business alike. It's all about weathering the storm while you grow and learning along the way. Look at me: I'm running a distillery despite having no official industry experience, and our flagship Chapter One London Dry gin has won an award in every competition we've entered. I've written a book having what I'd call *moderate* journalism experience.

## So, Why Gin?

I went to school for business, but I was convinced good grades only came from fabulous bullshit, so I learned to B.S. quite effectively for years, spending countless hours sifting through a thesaurus to make my essay answers seem that much better. Combine that with my hobby of reading great books and, apparently, I can write well enough to get published. Maybe I'll call my next book *50 Shades of Gin* and shoot for a bestseller list!

I'm simply writing about my experience. It would be a grossly inappropriate claim to call this a biography when I'm only thirty years old—or a dire premonition should this constitute my life in its entirety—but no matter what you call it, I hope it helps. I mean that sincerely. One of the best parts of this industry is that, for the most part, we all get along. The small producers know that we only make up two or three percent of the total market, so we know fighting isn't going to do any good. We get together for drinks, share trade secrets, and plot our takeover of a market dominated by huge players.

If you get overwhelmed, just pour yourself a Negroni and put life on pause for a moment. The traditional recipe calls for equal parts gin, Campari, and sweet vermouth, but I'd advise another half-part of gin. Stir briefly with ice and strain into a glass with one large ice cube. Peel an orange rind right over the drink so the lighter citrus oils fall into it, wipe the rim lightly with the peel, and drop it in. Oh, and use a barrel-aged gin. Trust me on this one, you don't have to stick with tradition all of the time.

Sometimes it's fun to take a risk and try something new.

## About the Author

AJ Temple is owner and head distiller for Temple Distilling, based in Lynnwood, Washington. They are the authors of Chapter One London Dry and Navy Strength Gins, Woodcut Barrel-Rested Gin, Bookmark Limoncello, and their limited Co-Authored series of unique dry gins made in collaboration with bartenders. Born and raised in the Pacific Northwest, AJ is married to his high-school sweetheart and co-conspirator Jamie who, according to him, keeps the lights on and tax collectors at bay. They have two young boys, Thomas and Eli, who unfortunately aren't yet old enough to peel lemons for limoncello, but Thomas does know how to recite the ingredients in a proper Negroni. They might be in trouble down the road.

www.ingramcontent.com/pod-product-compliance
Lightning Source LLC
Chambersburg PA
CBHW060211050426
42446CB00013B/3043